حضرة صاحب الجلالة الملك حمد بن عيسى آل خليفة
ملك مملكة البحرين المفدى

CAMBRIDGE UNIVERSITY PRESS
Cambridge, New York, Melbourne, Madrid, Cape Town, Singapore, São Paulo, Delhi

Cambridge University Press
The Edinburgh Building, Cambridge CB2 8RU, UK

www.cambridge.org
Information on this title: www.cambridge.org/9780521617857

First published 2006
Reprinted 2008

Printed in Dubai by Oriental Press.

A catalogue record for this publication is available from the British Library.

ISBN 978-0-521-69417-9 Workbook with Audio CD (Bahrain edition)
ISBN 978-0-521-69276-2 Student's Book (Bahrain edition)
ISBN 978-0-521-61317-0 Teacher's Book
ISBN 978-0-521-61318-7 Audio Cassette
ISBN 978-0-521-61319-4 Audio CD

BUSINESS GOALS 3

Contents

Amanda Thomas

WORKBOOK

CAMBRIDGE
UNIVERSITY PRESS

1 On the phone

Self-assessment: understanding telephone messages at work

1 How good are you at understanding telephone messages? Which statement is true for you? Put a tick or a cross in the box next to each statement 1–3.

☐ 1 I can understand most routine telephone messages if the caller speaks clearly and slowly.

☐ 2 I can understand routine telephone messages given at normal speed with only occasional misunderstandings.

☐ 3 I can confidently understand routine telephone messages and ask for clarification if necessary.

△TIP Developing an awareness of your strengths and weaknesses will help you to become a more independent learner by giving you a set of goals to work towards. For example, if you ticked statement 1, you need to be working towards achieving statement 2.

Listening focus 1: understanding connected speech

△TIP Understanding spoken English is sometimes difficult because it is different from written English. Remember the spoken form doesn't necessarily sound like the words written on the page.

2 a ⊙ Listen to the first part of the conversation and answer the questions.

1 Where is Oliver Richardson?

a Working at his desk

b Unavailable to answer the phone

2 What does Sarah say exactly?

a I'm afraid ....

b Can I .... ?

b ⊙ Listen again. Notice how the words are linked together in spoken English: *Not at* becomes /nɒtət/.

Listening focus 2: note-taking

3 a ⊙ **Listen to two conversations and complete the notes.**

Conversation One

Telephone message for: Oliver Richardson

Date: 12/09/04

Caller's name: Martin (1)

Company: The (2)

Calling about: (3) .... in October

Telephone number: (4)

Conversation Two

Message for: Chris Parnell

From: Frank (5)

Name of company: (6)

Wants to meet on: November (7)

Appointment time: (8) .... if possible

Telephone number: (9)

Mobile: 00466 2121378

b ⊙ **Listen to the conversations again. Then read and listen to the transcripts on page 64 to check your answers. Pay attention to the linking between words.**

⚠ TIP If you got any of the numbers or spellings wrong, do some more practice. Ask a friend to read out spellings, prices, dates and telephone numbers for you to write down.

Reading focus 1: understanding vocabulary

4 a **Look at the article below giving advice about cold calling. Tick the advice you think the article will mention.**

☐ When to call	☐ What information you should know before calling
☐ Where to make your calls	☐ What you should try to achieve
☐ How to make small talk	☐ What to do after your call
☐ How to start your call	

b **Read the article quickly and see if your predictions were correct.**

Effective cold calling

To any business at any stage, sourcing new sales leads and recruiting new customers is crucial. Cold calling potential customers is one way of generating new business. It's a direct marketing method that can also be a highly cost-effective sales (1) ....

However it's important to be well (2) .... to make your calls effective. First of all, you need somewhere quiet where you can (3) .... and where you won't be (4) ....

Experts say only one in five cold calls is effective, so the longer your prospect list, the more chance of (5) .... a sale. Check that names, job titles and (6) .... details are up to date before calling.

It's a good idea to plan your opening line because you need to (7) .... a good impression quickly. Introduce yourself and then get (8) .... to the point. Being on the phone can make your mind go blank, so have all (9) .... details in front of you such as: how much your goods or services cost; how many have already been sold and why your (10) .... is better than the competition's.

And finally, every call should result in (11) .... action, such as: (12) .... a sales appointment or sending out a brochure. Or even just crossing a name off your list, or agreeing to call back in a year's time.

c Read the article again. For each gap 1–12, circle the correct answer (A B, C or D).

1 A instrument	B machine	C tool	D object
2 A prepared	B provided	C presented	D programmed
3 A consider	B concentrate	C select	D persuade
4 A disconnected	B troubled	C interrupted	D interfered
5 A doing	B having	C taking	D making
6 A contact	B communication	C telephone	D connection
7 A make	B have	C get	D be
8 A openly	B clearly	C straight	D exactly
9 A related	B significant	C suitable	D relevant
10 A object	B project	C product	D plan
11 A getting	B doing	C taking	D following
12 A fixing	B deciding	C forming	D acquiring

5 Look at the sentences below. Which verbs go with these phrases?

take	make (x2)	get	generate

1 To .... a good impression   3 To .... a sale   5 To .... new business

2 To .... straight to the point   4 To .... action

Speaking focus: mini-presentations

6 a Look at the prompt card and make some notes.

b (○) Listen to a salesperson talking about cold calling and fill in the gaps with words from the box.

but	so	for example	obviously	or

WHAT IS IMPORTANT WHEN ...?

COLD CALLING
- Achieving your aims
- Preparing what to say
-
-

(1) .... it's important to try and achieve your aims when you're cold calling. It probably helps to have clear aims in mind for each call. (2) ...., getting the name of the right person to speak to from one company (3) .... to arrange a meeting. (4) .... I think you can use every call to find out more about potential customers; who the decision makers are, how interested they are, how big the company is and so on. (5) .... you shouldn't feel worried if you don't always achieve your main aims.

It's a good idea to prepare what you want to say before you call so that you don't forget anything important. However, you shouldn't prepare too well – it's important to sound natural on the telephone and not like you're reading from a script.

c Look at your notes again. Did you make any of the same points as the salesperson? Think of examples to support your ideas.

d Give a one minute presentation.

e Practise doing your mini-presentation two or three times until you can speak fluently. Make sure you use linking words to help organise your ideas.

Follow-up

Ask a partner to listen to your mini-presentation or record yourself.

Is it clearly organised?

Is your pronunciation clear?

Reading focus 2

 Read this letter about a marketing conference. There are some spelling mistakes and some extra words. Find and correct the errors. The first two have been done for you.

Dear Mr O'Sullivan

Further to our telephone conversation yesterday, I am ~~writting~~ *writing* to give you ~~a~~ more information about the MIS annual confrence.

The event will be take place on 22 Febuary at The Lancaster Hotel and is aimed at senior marketing personnel responsable for the branding and brand developement.

As you would expect it from the world's largest marketing organisation, we have arranged for some very well-known speekers so you should not to miss this oportunity.

Previuos conferences which have been oversubscribed, so you should apply for tickets now by completing in the inclosed booking form or by visiting our website.

Writing focus

 a You work for a company selling office equipment (PCs, fax machines, photocopiers, etc.). One of your best customers, Chris Johnson, has just returned from holiday. Write an email to Chris (between 40–50 words):

- asking about his holiday
- saying why you want to speak to him
- suggesting a date for a meeting.

Decide:
- how to start/close the email
- why you need to contact Chris
- what language you should use for making a suggestion.

b Check your email carefully for spelling and grammar mistakes.

Model answer ▶ *page 75*

2 Arrangements

Reading focus

1 a Read the short texts (A–D) about emails. Where do you think each text was taken from?

A magazine article   A report   An instruction manual

b Match texts A–D to statements 1–4 below.

1 emphasising why companies should deal with emails efficiently ☐

2 giving help on organising email correspondence ☐

3 reporting on the findings of a survey on email use at work ☐

4 complaining about the problems caused by increased email correspondence ☐

A

Email generally earns high marks in the workplace as a tool of communication, an aid in many work tasks, a facilitator of good working relationships, and even a source of pleasure and fun in the workplace. However, a small number of workers said that email in the workplace has made them too accessible to others, and can be a distraction or source of misunderstanding and additional stress. Workers generally behaved very responsibly with their email in the workplace, considering it a work tool. Only 5% of workers found spam to be a problem in their work-email inboxes.

B

Time management, the lack of effective communications and email overload are strangling our organisations and no one is solving the problem! I maintain that the majority of employees have shifted their goals from getting the job done, to getting through the day's emails, and their overloaded inbox. This is not simply a problem of poor time management.

While there are many ways to process emails more effectively using filters and auto-responders, better subject headings and clearer writing, it is only a matter of time before our new found capacity to process and manage these messages is exhausted.

C

Use filters to automatically prioritise your inbox. Assign each message a category (or label) based on what group the sender belongs to. If you assign categories in the order of their importance, then your inbox will list messages in the order you want to deal with them.

D

It is amazing to find that in this day and age, some companies have still not realised how important their email communications are. Many companies send email replies late, or not at all, or send replies that do not actually answer the questions you asked. If your company is able to deal professionally with email, this will help to provide that all important competitive edge. Moreover, by educating employees as to what can and cannot be said in an email, you can protect your company from awkward liability issues.

c Match the statements 1–7 to texts A–D. Underline the relevant phrases or sentences in each text.

1 How employees feel about using email ☐

2 A concern about future use of email ☐

3 A reason for taking care when writing emails ☐

4 Avoiding legal problems ☐

5 What to use to organise your inbox ☐

6 The effect increased email is having on workload ☐

7 Dealing with more urgent emails first ☐

Writing focus

2 **How good are you at dealing with business correspondence? Put a tick in the box next to the statement that is true for you.**

1 I can write simple, factual emails and letters but I make basic mistakes. ☐

2 I can deal with most routine correspondence with minimal errors. ☐

3 I can deal confidently with all types of business correspondence. ☐

⚠ TIP Careful planning is the first step to writing better emails and letters.

3 **Look at the spidergram for planning an email or letter. Fill in the gaps with the correct headings.**

Organisation	Reason for writing
Writing style	Target reader

1).................: what are the main points you need to make?

2).................: What information do they need? Should you write in a formal/informal style?

PLANNING

3).................: What is the best way to order the information?

4).................: Which greeting, signing off phrase, introductory/concluding sentence is it appropriate to use?

4 Read the email below and answer the questions.

  1 What is the email about?
  2 What information does Nick need?
  3 Is this email formal or informal?
  4 What do you think the relationship is between Josh and Nick?

> Hi Josh
>
> I'm organising a training day for senior staff on team leadership. This is so we can help team leaders to motivate their teams more effectively.
>
> I'd like to do this on 25 or 28 October. Can you give me your availability for these dates?
>
> Thanks
>
> Nick

5 You are a manager for a large bank and want to organise a meeting with an important client. You would like a colleague to attend the meeting with you. Write an email to your colleague (between 40–50 words):

  • explaining what the meeting will be about
  • explaining what you hope to achieve
  • checking availability.

TIP Before you write, look at Language Files 1 and 2 on page 86–87 of the Student's Book and choose the most appropriate language to use.

Plan your email carefully before you start writing.

Model answer ▶ *page 75*

Listening focus

6 a Match phrases 1–4 with the situations A–D.

  1 I'd be grateful if you could get back to me as soon as possible. ☐

  2 After careful consideration we have decided to go with another agency. ☐

  3 We really appreciate the fact that you've given up your time to be here today. ☐

  4 I'll have to check and get back to you. ☐

  A stalling a decision
  B rejecting a proposal
  C thanking a speaker
  D requesting action

  b Listen to four short recordings. What is the speaker doing (A–D) in each recording?

  c Check your answers by looking at the transcript on page 64. Underline phrases 1–4 in the transcript.

Speaking focus

7   a   ⊙ Listen to a manager being interviewed about email. What does he think would be the benefits of limiting the number of internal emails?

    b   What advantages and disadvantages does he mention?

Advantages	Disadvantages

    c   ⊙ Look at the transcript on pages 64–65. Listen again and read the interview. Underline where the speaker:

- gives examples
- uses fillers (*well*)
- hesitates
- repeats part of the question when answering
- repeats himself

    d   Practise answering the questions using your own ideas. If you have a partner, ask each other the questions.

- How much do you use email at work or in your studies?
- What advantages do you think there are for employees in using emails rather than letters?
- Do you think email has changed the way people work?
- Do you think there are any problems for companies using email?
- Have you experienced any problems using email?
- Do you think companies should try to control the number of internal emails that are sent?

3 | Effective communication

Writing focus

1 a Read the email from your manager, Jane Rogers. What does she want to introduce?

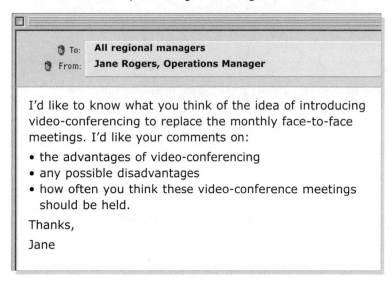

To: **All regional managers**

From: **Jane Rogers, Operations Manager**

I'd like to know what you think of the idea of introducing video-conferencing to replace the monthly face-to-face meetings. I'd like your comments on:

• the advantages of video-conferencing
• any possible disadvantages
• how often you think these video-conference meetings should be held.

Thanks,

Jane

b What do you think of this idea? Plan your reply to Jane. Make some notes.

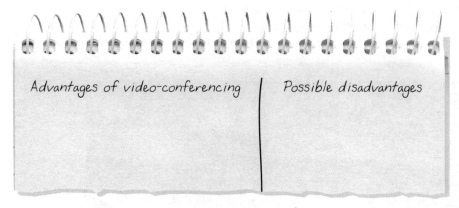

Advantages of video-conferencing | Possible disadvantages

c Write your reply to Jane Rogers (between 40–50 words).

Model answer ▶ *page 75*

TIP To be effective, a piece of written communication must:
• provide all the relevant information
• be well-organised
• have a good range of vocabulary and structure
• be accurate (no spelling or grammar mistakes)
• be written in an appropriate style.

Reading focus: understanding text structure

 a Look at the title of the article below. What do you think the text will give advice on?

- selecting team members
- joining a team
- cultural differences
- motivating a team
- equipment

b Read the article quickly to see if you were right. Don't worry about the missing sentences.

Managing virtual teams

Virtual teams are only possible because of advances in technology. But some organisations fail to make effective use of expensive video or telephone conferencing facilities because they let technology drive the team and not the other way round. (1)...
It's also essential to ensure that everybody, including team members from other organisations, has access to the same equipment and training.

Technology and distance can push a virtual team into focusing only on tasks. But research shows that high performing virtual teams spend more time on social interaction than weaker teams.
(2)...

This is especially important when team members come from different cultures; an awareness of cultural differences and an understanding of why people act as they do is essential. Team members may sometimes behave in an unexpected,

unpredictable way. (3)...
Many managers find it helpful to organise a team workshop on working across cultures to help understand these differences.

It's useful to consider the virtual team members as pieces of a jigsaw scattered over time and space. Each jigsaw piece is potentially useful for helping to see the bigger picture as each piece holds different information.
(4)...
Hence the manager's role may often be that of facilitator or coach rather than traditional manager.

(5)...
To avoid this, managers will need to keep reminding the team of its objectives in as many ways as possible. Managing performance in such teams requires good target setting and frequent monitoring because motivation is often harder to maintain than on a normal team.

c Read the article again. Choose the best sentence (A–E) to fill each of the gaps.

A With team members working at a distance, it can be easy to lose sight of goals.
B It's therefore important to choose appropriate (not necessarily the most advanced) systems for the team.
C Managers must learn to accept this and not to react negatively.
D Having knowledge distributed in this way means leadership may need to be taken on occasions by all members.
E Face-to-face meetings, although they may appear expensive, may actually save money in the long run.

 1 Read the article quickly to get a general understanding.

2 Underline the key words in each sentence (A–E). Does the meaning fit the ideas in the rest of the paragraph?

3 Look at the sentence before and after each gap. See if the linking words, tenses and pronoun references (this, it, them, etc.) fit.

Listening focus: opinions and suggestions

3 a Listen to a conversation between an operations manager and two members of a team, Sara and Camilla. What kind of team do they work in?

b Listen again. For each question 1–5 circle the correct answer (A, B or C.)

> **TIP**
> - Reading the questions will help you to focus on the information you need.
> - Questions 1–4 are testing your understanding of opinions, so listen carefully for language related to opinions.
> - Question 5 is about suggestions, so focus your attention on listening to the suggestions that are made.
> - Remember that the questions are often paraphrases of the words in the conversation, so it's important to listen for meaning – not specific words.

1 Sara and Camilla's team leader is good at

   A listening to other people.
   B giving advice.
   C making decisions quickly.

2 What do they say about the other people on their team?

   A They have similar ideas.
   B They know each other well.
   C They argue a lot.

3 What issue do Sara and Camilla disagree about?

   A the effectiveness of meetings
   B the time meetings take
   C how easy it is to keep informed

4 How do they think the team has changed over the last year?

   A They have clearer targets.
   B There are more frequent meetings.
   C The team is bigger.

5 How do Sara and Camilla think the team could be improved?

   A more socialising
   B more training
   C better equipment

c Look at the transcript on page 65 to check your answers. Underline the language used for:

| asking for opinions | agreeing | disagreeing |
| giving opinions | asking for suggestions | making suggestions |

14

Self-assessment: participating in groups

4 **a** Which statement is true for you? Put a tick or a cross in the box next to each statement.

☐ I can express my opinion adequately but I make a lot of mistakes.

☐ I have problems expressing my opinion because I don't know the right words.

☐ I find it difficult to play an active role during group discussions because I'm afraid of making mistakes.

☐ I don't usually participate and if asked for my opinion I can only give short answers.

b Match the statements to the TIPS (A–D) for improving speaking skills in group situations.

TIP A One way to build your confidence is to prepare very carefully before meetings and to rehearse exactly what you want to say. Asking questions will make it easier for you to participate more.

B Develop compensation strategies to help you express yourself e.g. Learn to paraphrase and simplify your language.

C Ask a teacher or partner to give you feedback to identify exactly what kind of language errors you are making.

D Thinking quickly in a foreign language is very difficult and needs a lot of practice. Accept that you will make some mistakes and don't give up.

Speaking focus: group discussions

5 **a** Read the following situation.

Effective communications

The IT company you work for feels there is a lack of communication between staff.
You have been asked to suggest ways of improving communications.

Discuss the situation together and decide:
• whether to introduce more social events
• whether to have more face-to-face meetings.

b Now make some notes:

IMPROVING COMMUNICATIONS	advantages	disadvantages
Face-to-face meetings		
Social events		
Other ideas?		

c ⊙ Listen to two managers discussing the same situation and complete these phrases for making suggestions, agreeing and disagreeing.

1 What .... having monthly briefing meetings?

2 I suppose ....

3 We .... it for a few months.

4 I'm not sure that ....

5 That's a ....

d Work with a partner. Discuss your ideas together.

4 Finding work

Reading focus 1

1 a Read the job advertisement quickly. What kind of experience is the company looking for?

Regional Retail Manager

As part of our regional sales team, you'll work (1)............. with colleagues to (2)............. partnerships with customers across your region. The successful candidate will be required to individually manage their region with the (3)............. of the regional sales director.
It will be your responsibility to (4) .... the challenge of increasing sales performance in a demanding and fast-moving environment.

Although you may not have (5)............. experience of working in the retail industry, you should have worked for 2 years in sales and have evidence you are driven by (6)............. results and developing successful relationships. You will also need to (7)............. a proven track record of problem solving and (8)............. customer service. Combined with natural sales skills, product awareness will also be (9)............. to your success. Candidates will also need to have good IT skills and, although not essential, education to degree level would be an (10)............. .

b Read the advertisement again. For each gap 1–10, circle the correct answer (A, B, C or D).

1	A tightly	B	closely	C	strongly	D	nearly
2	A make	B	expand	C	build	D	do
3	A knowledge	B	background	C	connection	D	support
4	A stay	B	meet	C	see	D	reach
5	A previous	B	real	C	first	D	earlier
6	A bringing	B	gaining	C	achieving	D	winning
7	A be	B	have	C	get	D	do
8	A creating	B	involving	C	progressing	D	improving
9	A necessary	B	vital	C	clear	D	useful
10	A necessity	B	improvement	C	advantage	D	ideal

⚠TIP To help you choose the correct word, read the whole sentence and pay attention to the words before and after each gap.

Decide what part of speech the missing word is. A noun? An adjective? A verb?

Is it part of a collocation or expression?

2 Each of the words below can also fit one of the gaps 1–10 in the text. Match the word to the correct gap.

asset   developing   face
co-operatively demonstrate   getting
crucial   direct   help
develop

Reading focus 2: editing

3 a Read the letter of application. Do you think Sharon is well qualified for the job?

b Read Sharon's letter again. There are seven extra words. Find them and delete them. The first one has been done for you.

⚠ **TIP** Try to get into the habit of checking your own work for accuracy.

> Dear Sir/ Madam
>
> I am writing to apply for the post of Regional Retail Manager as advertised in this week's Marketing News.
>
> You will see from my enclosed CV that I have a̶ three years experience as a sales rep. In the last two years I have been twice won the top sales rep award because for winning the most new contracts.
>
> Although I do not have a degree but I am currently studying for a diploma in marketing.
>
> I am very interested in this post because I am keen to pursue on a career in sales and feel I am ready to take on one more responsibility and would enjoy a new challenge.
>
> I am look forward to hearing from you soon.
>
> Yours faithfully
>
> Sharon Godard

Self-assessment: reading business texts

4 Which statement is true for you? Put a tick or a cross in the box next to each statement.

☐ I can understand business articles on familiar topics but I need to use a dictionary a lot.

☐ I can read and understand business texts on familiar topics but it takes me a long time.

☐ I can read most types of business texts quickly to understand the general meaning but I lack knowledge of specific business vocabulary.

⚠ **TIP** Use these reading strategies to increase your reading speed:

1 Predicting
Use clues (e.g. the title, pictures, names of people/companies) to help predict what the text is about. This will help you to focus on the main ideas.

2 Skimming
Read the text very quickly to get a general understanding. Try to guess the meaning of words from the context.

3 Reading groups of words together
Instead of reading each word individually, learn to recognise (and predict) patterns or groups of words. For example:

To keep up-to-date with
You will also be responsible for ...ing

Writing focus: writing reports

 Read this report. What is the problem? What course of action does it recommend?

Overcoming Recruitment Difficulties

Problem
Over the past year the company has found it difficult to recruit staff with the right experience and qualifications. In some cases no suitable candidates responded to job advertisements.

Possible solutions
Increasing starting salaries/other benefits
We do not feel this is the right action to take because our salaries/benefits are already competitive.

Recruiting staff from overseas
We feel this is an expensive option and we may find it difficult to recruit staff with good enough language skills.

Introduce an in-house training scheme
This is probably the best course of action to take. In this area there is not a labour shortage; our problem is finding staff with the right skills and experience. At the recruitment stage we need to identify staff with the potential to grow and then train them ourselves.

 Write a similar report on retaining managers.

- Your company is having problems retaining managers who joined the company as graduate trainees. Your line manager wants you to write a report explaining the reasons for this and suggesting possible solutions.
- Look at the information below, on which you have already made some handwritten notes.
- Write your report (between 120–140 words).

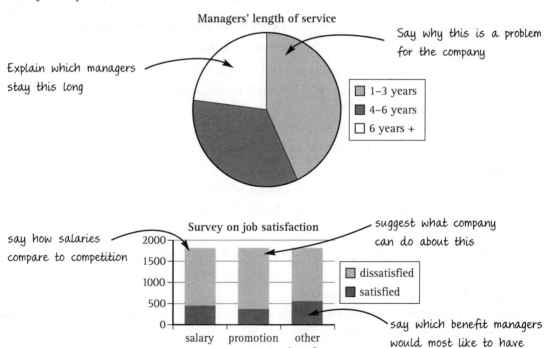

Model answer ▶ *page 76*

18

Listening focus: identifying functions

7 a ⊙ Listen to four short recordings about interviews. For each recording, decide if the speaker is talking to:

- colleagues
- a candidate
- an interviewer.

1 ....
2 ....
3 ....
4 ....

b ⊙ Listen again and decide what the speaker is doing (A–G).

A making a comparison
B making an offer
C making a decision
D explaining past actions
E requesting information
F making a recommendation
G giving an invitation

c Check your answers by looking at the transcript on page 66.

Speaking focus: mini-presentations

8 a Look at the prompt card and make some notes.

b Give a one minute presentation.

c ⊙ Listen to a Personnel Director talking about attending a job interview. Does she make the same points as you?

> **WHAT'S IMPORTANT WHEN ...?**
> Attending a job interview
> - asking questions
> - body language
> - •
> - •

d Look at the prompt cards and make some notes. Use ideas from the article on page 22 of the Student's Book to help you.

e Practise doing your presentation several times. Then do it in front of a partner if possible and ask them to give you feedback or record yourself and ask yourself these questions:

- Was it easy to understand?
- Did you speak too fast/slowly?
- Were your ideas well-organised?

> **WHAT'S IMPORTANT WHEN ...?**
> Attending a job interview
> - first impressions
> - being confident
> - •
> - •

5 | Working with others

Listening focus: asking permission/polite requests

1 a ◉ Listen to two conversations and complete the missing information on the forms below. Write one or two words or a number in the gaps.

Conversation One

Request for shift change

Name of employee: Leslie Smithson

Will change shift from: 25th April to **(1)**.................................

Will work on: **(2)**............................... shift

Reason for shift change: needs to go to **(3)**.................................

Person to swap shift: Anna **(4)**...............................

Conversation Two

Approval for training course

Training provider: (1) The .... Training Centre

Title of workshop: (2) ....

Venue: in office

Total cost: (3) £...

Suggested date: (4) .... October

b ◉ Listen again. Then check your answers by reading the transcript on page 66. Underline all the language for giving and refusing requests.

Follow-up

◉ Listen again and fill gaps 1–5 with the missing words.

1 .... I could have a word with you.
2 .... I joined you at eleven?
3 .... to finish the report by Friday?
4 .... if I let you know tomorrow?
5 .... check these figures for me?

Notice the intonation used to make requests more polite.

I was wondering if I could have a word with you.

Practise saying the requests politely using the correct intonation.

Reading focus

 a **Read texts A–D about delegating quickly.**

Which texts:

- provide advice?
- focus on the advantages of delegating?
- describe the personal qualities needed to be a good delegator?

A

Delegating responsibilities to those you trust would free you to focus on what you are best at. Delegating is a valuable tool for retaining and motivating your people. However, if current employees don't have the skills your business needs, don't hesitate to hire someone who does. It often makes sense to search for someone who can immediately add value to your management team as well as transfer some of his or her skills to others in your organisation.

B

Delegation develops the skills and capability of your people to enable them to assume greater responsibility. A routine task for you may be a growth opportunity for a team member and people perform at their best when they are challenged and stimulated to learn. Delegation also encourages team members to understand and influence the work done by everyone else in the team and to see the 'bigger picture'. When you delegate tasks according to the skills and abilities of each individual, the team will function at a higher and more efficient level. Delegation helps you to make the best use of available human resources and achieve the highest possible rate of productivity. In addition, it allows new ideas, viewpoints and suggestions to flourish.

C

Delegating does not mean forgetting about the task until the completion date so that it's too late to sort any problems out. When planning to delegate, time should be built in to review the process. Understanding the difference between interference and neglect is a skill which managers need to develop. Otherwise problems can result from being either too 'hands on' with well-motivated people, so that we demotivate them; or too 'hands off' with unenthusiastic people, so that we find out at the last minute that the task has been completed inadequately, or not at all.

D

In order to delegate effectively, you have to be confident. If you lack confidence, you may find it hard to give instructions and you'll put off delegating. If you do delegate, and problems arise because the employee fails to do what you've asked, you may doubt your own ability to confront the person about his or her actions. If staff have been given increased responsibilities and have done well, you may not be confident of being able to reward them sufficiently.

You might also be reluctant to delegate tasks that you think are too dull.

b Match statements 1–7 to texts A–D.

1 The importance of delegating tasks for the purposes of staff development.

2 The need to achieve the right balance in monitoring effectively.

3 The difficulties less experienced managers may find with delegating

4 The need to select appropriate people for the task.

5 The benefits of delegation for the organisation as a whole.

6 The reasons why some managers avoid delegation.

7 The fact that delegating allows managers to concentrate on their areas of expertise.

TIP

1 Underline the main idea in each sentence.

2 Scan the texts quickly to find words with similar meaning.

3 Underline the words in each text which match the sentences.

c Match the two halves of the phrases below. Check your answers by finding the fixed phrases in texts A and B.

1 to add	a the bigger picture
2 to achieve	b the best use of ...
3 to assume	c the highest rate of productivity
4 to make	d greater responsibility
5 to see	e value

Writing focus

3 You are a regional marketing manager working for an international company. You have arranged a business trip next month but now you cannot go and you want your assistant to go in your place. Write an email to your assistant, Eric Kleber (between 40–50 words):

• requesting that he goes on the trip
• explaining the purpose of the trip
• telling him to write a report when he gets back.

TIP

1 Plan carefully. Select appropriate information and organise your ideas.

2 Use appropriate language. (For this task, look at the language files on pages 86–88 and 95 in the Student's Book.)

3 Check for spelling and grammar mistakes.

Model answer ▶ *page 76*

Self-assessment: presentations

 4 Which statement is true for you? Put a tick or a cross in the box next to each statement.

☐ I can give very simple presentations in English but need to read out a prepared text or use detailed notes. I am not confident about answering questions.

☐ I can make short presentations in English using notes but I think I am sometimes difficult to understand because I make a lot of mistakes or because my pronunciation is not clear.

☐ I can confidently do short presentations in English from notes well enough for the listener to understand easily. I am able to answer questions adequately.

TIP To improve accuracy, fluency and gain confidence:

- Draw a mind-map. (see example below)
- Practise doing the mini-presentation a few times. Focus on linking your ideas and the pronunciation of any difficult words.
- Do the presentation in front of a teacher/ partner. Get them to ask you a question at the end. Then ask for feedback on organisation and accuracy.

Speaking focus: presentations

 5 a Look at the task card. Prepare a mini-presentation. Use the mind-map to help you.

> **WHAT'S IMPORTANT WHEN ...?**
> Delegating
> - providing clear instructions
> - monitoring
> -
> -

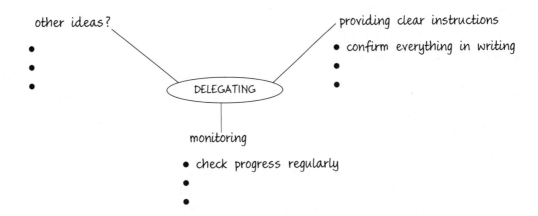

b Give a one minute presentation.

Model answer ▶▶ *CD track 21*

6 Performance at work

Listening focus: feedback

1 a ⊙ **Listen to four short recordings about performance reviews. For each recording, decide who is speaking:**

- the person giving feedback?
- the person receiving feedback?

1 .... 2 ....

3 .... 4 ....

b ⊙ **Listen again and decide what the speaker is doing (A–G).**

A apologising   E asking for clarification
B accepting criticism F making a recommendation
C giving advice   G giving reasons
D offering a solution

c Check your answers by reading the transcript on page 67.

Reading focus: vocabulary

a Skim read the report. Do you think Mike will be pleased with his performance review?

Performance Review Report

Employee: Stevenson, Mike
Job Title: New Products Manager

Leadership: needs improvement

Mike quickly (1)............... a strong leadership role when action is needed. He influences others to perform better. However, he would be a stronger leader if he (2)............... greater confidence in himself. Occasionally, his actions have resulted in a lack of (3)............... and trust from others. Mike has sometimes reacted poorly when put (4)............... pressure.

Teamwork: exceeds requirements

Mike gives clear, (5)............... feedback to team members and, in turn, actively requests feedback from them. He is successful in (6)............... his team and provides plenty of support. All his actions are directed towards achieving the (7)............... of the team as a whole. He demonstrates a high degree of openness to the views of others. Mike has been able to (8)............... the needs of his team with the needs of the company.

Delegation: meets requirements

Mike actively uses delegation to manage his (9)............... more effectively. He usually (10)............... tasks to people based on their skills, experience, strengths, and limitations, although his subordinates are often not (11)............... enough authority and independence to carry out these tasks. When Mike delegates work, he needs to be clearer in (12)............... goals and needs to (13)............... those activities regularly. Furthermore, he sometimes does not adequately recognise or give (14)............... to people for the results of work he has delegated.

---

b Read the report again. For each gap 1–4, circle the correct answer (A, B, C or D).

1 A takes	B expects	C prefers	D allows
2 A emphasised	B presented	C modelled	D displayed
3 A belief	B duty	C respect	D responsibility
4 A under	B below	C beneath	D against
5 A connected	B productive	C profitable	D constructive
6 A progressing	B motivating	C working	D winning
7 A decisions	B targets	C purposes	D directions
8 A balance	B compare	C answer	D maintain
9 A jobs	B roles	C workload	D range
10 A acquires	B assigns	C assesses	D deals
11 A participate	B helped	C taken	D given
12 A setting	B putting	C preparing	D arranging
13 A control	B monitor	C guide	D manage
14 A time	B congratulations	C credit	D acceptance

Language focus

3 Put the verbs in the correct circle to make collocations. You may use each verb more than once.

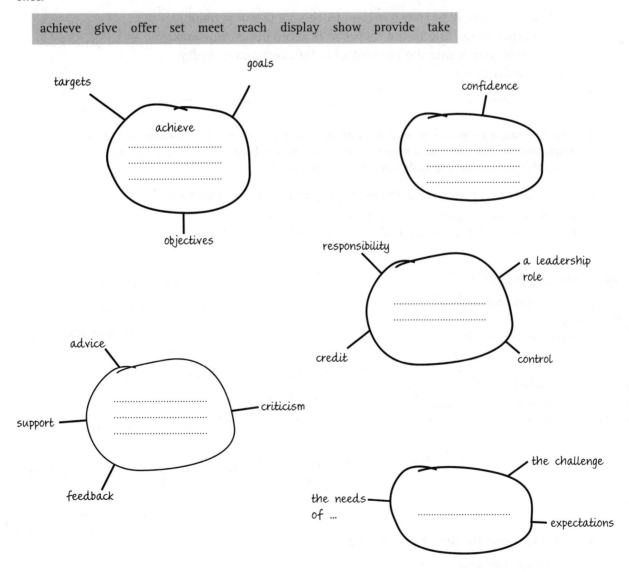

achieve   give   offer   set   meet   reach   display   show   provide   take

targets — goals — achieve — objectives

confidence

responsibility — a leadership role — credit — control

advice — criticism — support — feedback

the needs of … — the challenge — expectations

Writing focus: report writing

 a Read the performance report about Alica Hines, a temporary personal assistant. List all her qualities and skills.

> **PERFORMANCE REPORT: ALICIA HINES**
>
> **Job title: Temporary personal assistant**
>
> Although Alicia was only with us for a few months, she quickly established herself as part of the team. Alicia is hard-working and very organised and always willing to help others. Her organisational skills were particularly useful during the relocation of our office to the ground floor; Alicia managed to set the new office up very quickly.
>
> Alicia's professional skills are of a very high standard. She has excellent IT skills and she was also able to deal with daily business correspondence with very little supervision required. The presentation of her letters and reports was always very good.
>
> Alicia's knowledge of French proved to be very useful in helping us to organise our trip to the trade fair in Lyons earlier this year. I was able to delegate the booking of hotels, cars and meetings with clients to her.

b Jana Bowman, a temporary member of staff, is leaving your office. The recruitment agency which sent her has asked for a report on her performance. Look at the information below on which you have already made some handwritten notes.

c Plan a report reviewing Jana's performance using all your handwritten notes.

- Underline the important information you need to include.
- Use your imagination to think of relevant examples and comments.

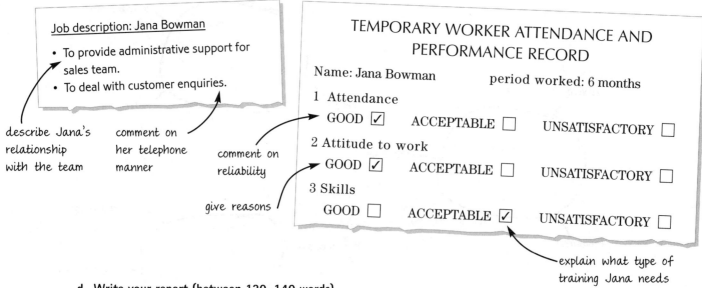

Job description: Jana Bowman
- To provide administrative support for sales team.
- To deal with customer enquiries.

describe Jana's relationship with the team

comment on her telephone manner

comment on reliability

give reasons

TEMPORARY WORKER ATTENDANCE AND
PERFORMANCE RECORD

Name: Jana Bowman   period worked: 6 months

1 Attendance
GOOD ☑   ACCEPTABLE ☐   UNSATISFACTORY ☐

2 Attitude to work
GOOD ☑   ACCEPTABLE ☐   UNSATISFACTORY ☐

3 Skills
GOOD ☐   ACCEPTABLE ☑   UNSATISFACTORY ☐

explain what type of training Jana needs

d Write your report (between 120–140 words).

Model answer ▶ *page 77*

Self-assessment: review your performance in English

 Which statement is true for you? Put a tick or a cross in the box next to each statement.

1 I am making an effort to record and learn new vocabulary. ☐

2 When I make a mistake in writing, I try to make sure I understand why it is wrong. ☐

3 I try to listen to business news in English at least once a week. ☐

4 I try to read articles/advertisements in English from business magazines at least once a week. ☐

5 I know what my strengths and weaknesses are in English. ☐

6 I think my .... is improving.

7 My target for the next month is to ....

Speaking focus: discussion

 a **The company you work for is thinking of introducing a reward scheme for staff who perform well. You have been asked to make recommendations. First think about:**

- what the advantages are for the company
- what kind of rewards to offer
- how to make this idea popular with employees.

b Discuss these points with a partner.

c ⊙ **Listen to two colleagues discussing the same situation. Do they have the same ideas as you?**

d Look at the transcript on page 67. Match the underlined examples where one colleague:

- expands on what their partner has just said
- asks for clarification
- responds positively to what their partner says.

⚠️ TIP Remember to:
- ask your partner for their opinion
- respond to what your partner says.

Reading focus: understanding text purpose and structure

1 **a** Read the article quickly and put a tick in the box beside the correct answer.

1 Who was it written by?

☐ a journalist

☐ a search engine user

☐ a Google employee

2 Who was it written for?

☐ website owners

☐ Google users

☐ general readers

3 What do you think the writer's purpose is in this article?

to persuade ☐   to inform ☐   to criticise ☐   to request ☐   to analyse ☐   to explain ☐

GOOGLE'S PAGE INDEX DOUBLES

[1] You probably never notice the large number that appears in tiny type at the bottom of the Google home page, but I do. It's a measure of how many pages we have in our index and gives an indication of how broadly we search to find the information you're looking for.
(1).. . That made me smile.

[2] Comprehensiveness is not the only important factor in evaluating a search engine, but it's certainly important when you are looking for information on a subject that only returns a few results. For example, now, when I search on behalf of friends who previously only generated a handful of results, I see double that number. (2).. The same is true for specialist topics, where you're now significantly more likely to find a wide range of relevant information about the subjects. You may also notice that the number of results for general queries has gone up substantially.

(3).. By constantly looking for ways to increase the efficiency of our serving environment, Google has broken its own speed records time and again.

[3] The documents in Google's index are in dozens of file types from HTML to PDF, including PowerPoint, Flash, PostScript and JavaScript. Together these pages represent a good chunk of the world's information, but hardly all of it. That's why we keep building more advanced systems for crawling the web and creating more sophisticated indices to sort what we find.
(4).. The real test is how well we do in finding what you want from within those pages. We'll keep improving that too because it's our mission to always deliver more than expected. For us, being the best is just a starting point.

b Read the article again and match statements A–D to paragraphs 1–3.

A Technical information about Google's service.
B Google announces new record.
C Google's aims.
D Three different ways in which Google's service has improved.

 Identifying the type of text (who wrote it, who it was written for) will help you understand the writer's purpose and the text as a whole. Depending on the type of text, the writer may have more than one purpose.

c Read the article again. For each gap 1–4 choose one of the missing sentences A–G. Do not use any sentence more than once.

A And we've achieved these results not through TV ad campaigns, but through word of mouth from one satisfied user to another.
B Today that number nearly doubled to more than 8 billion pages.
C These are not just copies of the same pages, but truly diverse results that give more information.
D Google is continuing to pioneer new technologies.
E So 8 billion pages is an achievement worth noting, but it's not the end of the road.
F Sometimes it was just a matter of integrating new databases, such as adding a phone number and a business directory.
G It's also got a lot faster.

TIP

1 Decide what kind of information is missing:
- an example?
- further information?
- a new piece of information?
- a summary of the main idea?

2 Identify the missing sentences which contain relevant information.

3 Look for sentences which fit grammatically. For example, do the pronoun references match (e.g. they/them)?

4 After matching all the sentences, read the text through to check it makes sense.

Writing focus: writing a paragraph

 a **Read the text below about improving listening skills in English.
In most lines there is one extra word. It is either grammatically correct or does not fit in
with the sense of the text. Underline the extra words.**

> I think the most best way to improve your English is to listen to as much
> of the language as possible. Obviously, this is much easier if you are live
> in an English-speaking environment or work with the English-speaking
> colleagues but if this is not the case, you can still listen to the radio,
> watch TV and you listen to all kinds of information on the Internet. I find
> that listening to business news very helpful because the same vocabulary
> is used again and again so that gradually you are begin to recognise the
> words even more easily. I prefer to learn vocabulary this way, rather than
> studying lists, which can be quite boring. Also like these reports tend to
> be quite short, focusing on one main idea, which means you don't have
> to concentrate for very long. Although listening to all reports on the radio
> or a television is quite different from listening to a discussion in a
> meeting, it does help in to prepare you for this situation by increasing
> your familiarity with different accent types and with the speed at which
> people speak.

b **Write a similar text agreeing with one of the opinions below.
First select relevant points and examples. Then use the structure below to
help organise your ideas.**

- It's important to take responsibility for your own learning.
- Learning vocabulary is more important than learning grammar.
- The best way to improve your English is by reading.
- Preparing for an English language test helps students to make faster progress.
- Living in or visiting an English-speaking country will improve your English.

Structure

Statement ....

Reason for opinion ....

(Further information) ....

Example ....

Concluding sentence ....

Self-assessment: listening to business news

3 Which statement is true for you? Put a tick or a cross in the box next to each statement.

☐ I can only understand a few words in business reports on TV/radio.

☐ I can understand the general meaning of news reports if I am familiar with the subject.

☐ I can understand detailed information about business reports on familiar subjects.

☐ I can follow business reports on any subject.

⚠️ TIP Try to listen to business news reports in English regularly. You will find they gradually become easier to understand. You will also learn useful vocabulary this way.

Listening focus

4 a 🔘 Listen to the business news extracts. Decide if the news is about:

- one company
- an industry sector
- customers.

b 🔘 Listen again and decide what the news is about (A–G).

A Announcing a new strategy.
B Describing a new product.
C Explaining why customer numbers have dropped.
D Launching a new service for customers.
E Comparing services by different providers.
F Reporting on changes in consumer behaviour.
G Re-structuring a company.

c Check your answers by looking at the transcript on page 68.

Follow-up

Did you get any answers wrong?

Remember for each correct answer there is also at least one distractor which contains similar language or information. For example:

The distractors for recording 1 are D or G. Both are wrong because the Internet service mentioned isn't a new service and although the company has recently had a lot of problems and has bought another company, these are not the main focus of the news item.

Speaking focus: giving opinions

5 a Discuss these questions with a partner. Try to give reasons for your opinions and support your arguments with examples.

- How do you use the Internet for work purposes?
- How do you think the Internet has changed the way people work?
- What advantages do you think the Internet has brought to smaller companies?
- Are there any disadvantages for customers in using the Internet?

b Listen to a product development manager answering the same questions. Does she make the same points as you?

8 Meetings

Listening focus: note-taking

1 a ◉ **Listen to two conversations and complete the missing information in the notes below. Write one or two words or a number in the gaps. Play the conversation twice.**

Conversation One

Marketing review meeting
Date: (1) .... April
Time: 10 am-1 p.m.
Place: (2) .... room
New item for agenda: (3) ....
Apologies sent by: (4) .... Spencer

Conversation Two

Credit Control Management Meeting
Date of next meeting changed to (5)....................
Thomas Hanson on leave. Ann Simpson will be acting (6)................
Brief Ann on (7)....................
Send Ann copy of (8)....................

TIP 1 Look at the notes before you listen and try to predict the type of missing information required.
2 Write down all possible answers the first time you listen.
3 If you miss an answer move on to the next one.
4 Confirm your answers during the second listening.
5 Check your spelling.

b Check your answers by reading the transcript on page 68.

Writing focus: choosing an appropriate style

2 a **You have to change the date of a meeting with a colleague, Laura Smith. You asked your assistant to write an email to Laura:**

- suggesting a different date
- giving a reason for the change of date
- requesting confirmation that she can attend.

What is wrong with the email your assistant has written?

b **Rewrite the email in a more appropriate style and including all the relevant information.**

c **Check your email:**

- Have you answered all the points?
- Does it make sense?
- Are there any grammar or spelling mistakes?
- Have you repeated words instead of using pronouns (this, it, etc.)

Model answer ▶ *page 78*

Dear Laura

What about a meeting on the 21st? I need to change the meeting date. It is now on the 21st February. The reason for changing the date of the meeting is because there is a problem with the other date.

Reading focus: reading for detailed information

 a Look at the review below of a book called *Death by Meetings*. Predict what you think the book is about. Choose from statements A–C.

A A description of what is wrong with meetings
B How to make meetings more effective
C Why it is better not to have meetings

b Read the article quickly to see if your prediction was correct.

Death by Meetings by Patrick Lencioni

Mary Ann Maxwell

My mind wanders as I sit through another long and boring meeting. I start to think about how much of my life I spend in meetings. Taking a rough estimate of 10 meeting hours a week, I calculate I will sit through more than 20,000 hours of meetings in my business career – that's more than 800 days.

I once worked for a company that banned meetings during business hours in an attempt to improve productivity. This was attractive at first but we soon found that sitting down in person with members of your group really is the most effective way to accomplish many tasks.

There are several advantages to meetings. One is that it's almost always harder and more time-consuming to convince someone of something by email than face-to-face, when you can react immediately to any opposition. Another is that problems requiring the knowledge and experience of several people often can be solved best by bringing them all together in a meeting. It is also the best way of involving others in taking responsibility for solving problems and making decisions. That involvement is the most effective way to ensure that people will accept and support a solution. So, why, I ask myself, do most of us react so negatively to the idea of meetings?

In *Death by Meetings* by Patrick Lencioni (Jossey-Bass 2004), the author argues that to make meetings more effective, we need to have a range of regular meetings with clearly defined purposes, formats and timings so that less time is wasted and everyone knows what to expect. For example, 'The Daily Check-in' requires that team members get together at the start of the day, standing up, to report on their activities for that day. It's a great way to keep everyone informed about what's going on. At 'The Monthly Strategic Meeting', teams meet to decide how to resolve problems. 'The Off-Site Review' provides senior managers with the opportunity to step away from the daily, weekly, even monthly issues for a couple of days so they can discuss their business more objectively, share ideas and set targets for the long-term.

If the time you currently spend in meetings is wasted, Lencioni believes the solution is not to stop having meetings, but to make them better. For those of us who lead organisations, this is not just an opportunity to improve the performance of our companies – it is also a way to have a positive effect on the working lives of our people. And that includes us.

c Read the review again. For each question 1–6, circle the correct answer (A, B, C or D).

1 The writer says that banning meetings during office hours

   A made the company more productive.
   B encouraged team members to talk to each other more.
   C made staff realise the value of meetings.
   D made it easier for staff to get their work done.

2 What comparison does the writer make between meetings and email?

   A It is easier to put your arguments across in meetings.
   B In meetings people are able to face problems immediately.
   C It takes more time to decide things in meetings.
   D Email gives people more time to think.

3 What does the writer say about decision-making?

A People may reject a decision if they are not involved in the decision-making process.
B More than one person should take responsibility for decisions.
C Everyone's ideas should be accepted and supported.
D It's easier to solve problems with more people involved.

4 In the book *Death by Meetings*, Lencioni recommends

A having shorter meetings.
B setting strict time limits on meetings.
C having a variety of meeting types.
D having meetings less frequently.

5 Lencioni says the 'Off-Site Review' meeting should

A be held as often as necessary.
B be used to plan the company's strategy.
C deal with recent difficult issues.
D set immediate targets.

6 The writer thinks Lencioni's ideas will

A be used in leading organisations.
B be difficult to achieve.
C make people work harder.
D bring benefits for everybody in the company.

 • Underline the key words in both the questions and the parts of the text that relate to each question.

• Look for words in the options (A, B, C and D) and the text which have similar meanings.

• Don't choose an option just because it has the same words as the text. Often you have to understand a whole paragraph to get the answer – not just one or two words.

Self-assessment: meetings

4 **Which statement is true for you? Put a tick or a cross in the box next to each statement.**

☐ It's difficult to follow what people say in meetings.

☐ I usually just listen to other people in meetings.

☐ I can participate in meetings, but need time to think about what to say.

☐ I like talking in meetings, but sometimes make a lot of mistakes.

TIP One way to take a more active role in meetings is to ask questions.

Speaking focus: discussion

5 a Read the following scenario and prepare some ideas for the discussion. You can use ideas from page 40 of the Student's Book to help you.

Improving meetings

Managers at your company frequently complain that too much time is wasted in meetings and that people don't stick to the agenda.

You have been asked to make some recommendations to improve the situation.

Discuss the situation with your partner and decide:

- how to make meetings more effective
- how to change staff behaviour in meetings.

Make some notes before you start.

How to make meetings more effective	How to change staff behaviour in meetings

b **Have a discussion with your partner. Try to talk for about three minutes.**

Model answer ▶ *CD track 34*

Writing focus: proposals

1 You work in the HR department of a bank and you want to arrange a course for new managers on time management. Look at the flyer about Rise Training and the email about Intrain on which you have already made some handwritten notes. Complete the proposal opposite using all your handwritten notes.

has a good reputation

RISE TRAINING

Britain's largest training organisation

Time Management Workshops

Course content includes:
- Managing workload
- Learning to say 'no'
- Introduction to stress management
- Managing pressure
- Techniques for dealing with distraction

competitive prices

Duration 1 day
Cost   £75
Location and dates: London   Sept 30 *full*
                      Birmingham Oct 2
                      Cardiff   Oct 11

explain why not convenient

these courses are too late

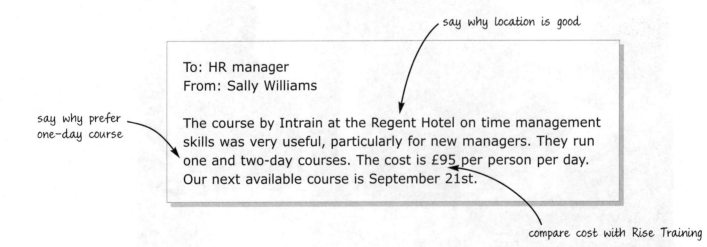

say why location is good

To: HR manager
From: Sally Williams

The course by Intrain at the Regent Hotel on time management skills was very useful, particularly for new managers. They run one and two-day courses. The cost is £95 per person per day. Our next available course is September 21st.

say why prefer one-day course

compare cost with Rise Training

Time Management Workshops for new managers

Proposal

Introduction
Training workshops by two training organisations were investigated: *Rise Training* and *Intrain*.

Rise Training
Advantages:
- This is a large training organisation with regular workshops on time management.
- Costs are competitive at £75 per person.

Disadvantages:
- Although the courses are run frequently, they are not conveniently located for us.
- Their next course is full and our managers need to attend as soon as possible.

Intrain
Advantages:

Disadvantages:

Recommendations:

Model answer ▶ *page 78*

Self-assessment: writing a proposal

2 Which statement is true for you? Put a tick or a cross in the box next to each statement.

☐ I included all the content points using the handwritten notes.

☐ I organised the information logically.

☐ I did not make any basic errors.

☐ I tried to use a range of structures and vocabulary.

Reading focus

3 a **Read the article on page 38 about a personal time management course.**

Who is this course for?

A People who don't like taking time off from work.
B People who want to improve on working as part of a team.
C People who want to get promoted more quickly.

b **Read the article again. For each gap 1–5, choose the correct sentence A–G.**

A They may start to think that your career is more important than they are.
B Our personal time management course will help you to choose what to do first, what to do second and what not to do at all.
C So concentrate on working when you are at work so that you can concentrate on your family when you are at home.
D It starts by asking you to think about what is really important to you in life.
E However, at home and in your personal life you can exercise a tremendous amount of control over how you use your time.
F To do this you need to have a clear vision of the skills and abilities you need to succeed at work.
G Instead of clearly deciding what you want to do, you continually react to what is happening around you.

Read the whole text underlining the main ideas in each paragraph and the missing sentences.
Look for lexical and grammatical clues, e.g. words with similar meanings, pronouns, plurals, tenses.

How to make Personal Time Management work for you

Perhaps the greatest single problem that people have today is 'time poverty'. Working people have too much to do and too little time for their personal lives. Most people feel overwhelmed with responsibilities and activities, and the harder they work, the further behind they feel. This sense of being on a never-ending treadmill can cause you to fall into a 'reactive' mode of living. (1).. Pretty soon you lose all sense of control. You feel that your life is running you, rather than you running your life.

Our personal time management course begins with you. (2)..
This includes specific personal life goals that you want to accomplish. These are the reasons why you get up in the morning, why you work hard and upgrade your skills, why you worry about money and sometimes feel frustrated by the demands on your time.

The second area of goals are your business and career goals. These are the 'how' goals, the means by which you achieve your personal, 'why' goals. It means working out how you can achieve the level of income that will enable you to fulfil your personal goals and how you can progress in your career. (3).. The course will help you identify these areas and how to achieve a satisfactory work-life balance.

A principle of time management says that 'hard' time pushes out 'soft' time. This means that 'hard' time, such as working, will push out 'soft' time, such as the time you spend with your family. If you don't get your work done because you don't use your time well, you invariably have to rob that time from your family. (4).. And you will feel stressed and irritable because you haven't been able to achieve a satisfactory work-life balance. Learning how to prioritise and plan will help you to overcome these problems.

(5).. It will help you to organise every aspect of your life so that you can get the greatest joy, happiness, and satisfaction out of everything you do.

c Would you find this course useful? Have you identified your personal and career goals?

Language focus

4 Match the words/phrases to the correct meaning.

1 treadmill (para 1)   a area
2 overwhelmed (para 1)   b repetitive/difficult work
3 upgrade (para 2)   c not able to cope
4 aspect (para 5)   d improve

Speaking focus

 a Think about your answers to the following questions. Support your answers with reasons and examples.

- Do you try to plan your work schedule in advance?
- How useful do you think it is for companies to organise time management training for their staff?
- Do you think people work more effectively when they have to meet a deadline?
- How important do you think it is for companies to make sure staff have a good work-life balance?

b **Listen to a colleague asking another colleague the questions. Summarise her answers.**

c Discuss the questions with a partner.

Listening focus: understanding detailed information

 a ⊙ **Listen to Peter Hall talking to his business adviser about time management. What are his two main problems?**

b Listen again. For each question, 1–5, circle the correct answer (A, B or C).

TIP

- Before you listen, read all the questions carefully and underline the key words. This will help you to focus on the information you need.
- Listen for the meaning not specific words. The words on the page may be paraphrases of the words the speakers use on the recording.

1 What does Peter say about his business trips?

  A They are usually a waste of time.
  B It's impossible to know in advance which ones will be useful.
  C He would like to make fewer trips in future.

2 The advisor says useful business trips are ones which involve

  A building better business contacts.
  B meeting large numbers of people.
  C staying in one location.

3 What does Peter say about using travelling time more productively?

  A He already works while he is travelling.
  B It would be possible to use the time more productively.
  C He thinks it's better to use that time to relax.

4 For dealing with a larger task while travelling, the advisor tells him to

  A divide the task into separate smaller tasks.
  B delegate as much as possible to other people.
  C spend 30 minutes each day working on it.

5 Peter thinks the advisor's suggestion for dealing with larger projects

  A will improve his organisational skills.
  B will save a lot of time.
  C may not be appropriate for all tasks.

c ⊙ **Check your answers by reading the transcript on page 69. Underline the parts which gave you the answers.**

d Look at the transcript on page 69. Underline the phrasal verbs with *get*.
Now fill the gaps with the correct word.

behind   back   down   on

1 Get .... to something –
to start doing something again

2 Get .... to work –
to start working seriously

3 Get .... with a task –
to continue working

4 Get .... with work –
to find it difficult to keep to deadlines

10 Advertising

Reading focus: reading for detail

 a Read the short extracts, A–D, on brands and advertising.

Which extracts mention:

- the importance of brands?
- a problem with advertising?

b Look at the statements 1–7 and decide which extract (A–D) each statement refers to.

1 How a brand can influence a workforce.
2 Some information about the behaviour of advertisers.
3 Why customers prefer buying well-known brands.
4 What contributes to making a successful brand.
5 An opinion on what should influence a company's decisions.
6 A claim that advertising does not always work.
7 A positive view about new advertising methods.

A

'Consumers are getting harder to influence as commercial clutter invades their lives', says a recent report by Deutsche Bank. It examined the effectiveness of TV advertising on 23 new and mature brands of packaged goods and concluded that in some cases it was a waste of time. In almost every case, there was only a positive cash return on that investment in 18% of cases. Over a longer term the picture improved, with 45% of cases showing a return on investment. Not surprisingly, new products did better than older ones.

B

Small and mid-sized businesses are still not advertising online, although most say they believe the Internet presents big advertising opportunities, according to a new report presented by local market research firm the Marlow Group. The report, presented at the Marlow Group's interactive local media conference, concluded that 61% of small and mid-sized enterprises believe the Internet is a significant advertising medium, but that only 14% of local businesses have advertised online in the last year.

C

Brands give potential customers a firm idea of what they're buying before they buy
it, making the purchasing decision easier. And existing customers trust strong brands
because they know exactly what to expect – and always get it.

Strong brands are those that stand out from the crowd, particularly in competitive
markets, where brands that deliver consistent messages to potential customers in
their advertising, both traditional and online and in every other point of contact with
customers, are usually the most successful. Advertising is therefore critical to create
a strong brand image and to make sure consumers receive a consistent message.

D

The significance of the Sony brand can be summed up by this quote from the
chairman of the board, Norio Ohga: 'In April of every year a large number of new
employees join the company. And what I always say to them is that we have many
marvellous assets here. The most valuable asset of all is the four letters, S, O, N, Y.
I tell them, make sure the basis of your actions is increasing the value of these four
letters. In other words, when you consider doing something, you must consider
whether your action will increase the value of SONY, or lower its value.'

Self-assessment: learning vocabulary

2 **Which statement is true for you? Put a tick or a cross in the box next to each statement.**

☐ I can only learn new words by writing them down and memorising them.

☐ I can usually guess the meaning of new words from the context before I check them in a dictionary.

☐ I can often pick up new words from reading texts or by hearing them on the radio/TV.

☐ I keep an organised list of new vocabulary.

⚠️ **TIP** Using spidergrams to record
vocabulary can help you to remember
not just one word but many of the
verbs/nouns/adjectives that usually
go with it (collocations).

strong, powerful,
weak, mature,
quality

create a brand
image

brand

increase brand value

raise brand
awareness

3 **Look at the words below. Which of these words collocate with *launch*?**

| an advertising campaign | a product | a missile | a schedule | an aeroplane | a ship |
| a space rocket | a train | a business | an attack | a presentation | a website | an idea |

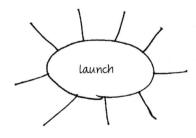

Reading focus: editing

 Read the article below. In some lines there is one extra word. It is either grammatically incorrect or does not fit in with the sense of the text. The first one is done for you. There are also eight spelling mistakes. Can you find them?

Skandia celebrates sponsorship of Cowes Week

This summer, a financial services company Skandia celebrated a decade as sponsor of one of the world's best-known sailing events, Cowes Week. This is an event which Skandia believes so represents its own brand values. Tim Sewell, Skandia's sponsorship manager explains: 'Cowes is all about the passion, courage and committment and that's very much what we want to say about ourselves as an organisation.'

The audiance at Cowes also are closely match Skandia's target customers. A recent survey of Cowes Week spectaters did showed that 60 per cent of respondents were likely to use an indipendent financial adviser in the future, compared to the national average of 22% each. In 2003, Skandia comissioned an independent evaluashion of the media exposure of the brand also at Cowes Week and concluded them that they acheived an impressive 300% return on investment. Figures like these too explain Skandia's desicion to continue sponsoring this event.

Listening focus: identifying context

 a ⦿ Listen to four short recordings about marketing. For each recording, decide whether the speakers are talking about marketing:

A for a specific product or company
B in general.

b ⦿ Listen again and decide what each speaker is doing (A–H).

1 ....
2 ....
3 ....
4 ....

A describing a product launch
B reviewing methods of advertising
C describing target customers
D describing an advertising campaign
E describing product values
F rejecting market research
G choosing a brand name
H comparing different brands

<u>TIP</u> Listen for the meaning. Don't choose an answer just because some of the words appear in both the option and the recording.

c Look at the transcript on page 70.

Speaking focus: mini-presentation

 a Look at the prompt card and make some notes.

b Read the mini-presentation below and underline the correct word in italics.

c ⊙ Listen and check your answers.

> **WHAT'S IMPORTANT WHEN CHOOSING A BRAND NAME?**
> • Image
> • Research
> •
> •

The first thing to consider when choosing a brand name is the *style/image* you want to create. Do you want a name that suggests your product is high-class, sleek and sophisticated or one that suggests it's *compatible/innovative* and exciting? You also have to have a clear idea about what the name can do for the product and what impact you want it to have on *potential/identified* customers. Do you want to surprise them or make them feel relaxed?

You should research the name carefully to make sure no-one else is using it and you need to find out if the name will travel well. You don't want to end *out/up* with a name that means something completely different in another language. A lot of companies use focus groups to try *on/out* new names but it's hard for *researchers/consumers* to say whether they like a name if they don't know much about the product and they haven't seen the logo or packaging.

It's very important to get your name trademarked so that the name legally belongs to your company. Then no-one else is allowed to use it. Sometimes you may find that the name is already being used and this means holding *on/up* the whole project until another name is chosen.

d What other point does the speaker mention apart from image and research? Add it to the prompt card.

e Give a one minute presentation.

Pronunciation: word stress

 a Put the words into the correct columns.

| affordable | potential | compatible | comprehensive | consumer |
| important | innovative | researcher | reliable | sophisticated |

1 ∘●●	2 ●∘∘∘	3 ∘●∘∘	4 ∘∘●∘	5 ∘●∘∘∘

b ⊙ Listen and check your answers.

11 Trading

Listening focus

1 a ⊙ Listen to the recording and write down the numbers/letters you hear.

1 ....

2 ....

3 ....

4 ....

5 ....

b ⊙ Listen to two telephone conversations about orders and complete the notes. Write one or two words or a number in each space.

Conversation One

ORDER FORM

Company name:	Simpson's
Account number:	(1)
Company address:	Black's Furniture Warehouse
	(2) Lowick LW5 6PQ
Description of goods:	Riviera kitchen units
Reference number:	(3)
Size:	(4) by 600 mm
Date for delivery:	(5)

Conversation Two

CUSTOMER SERVICE

Caller's name:	Martin Wright
Name of company:	(6)
Items ordered:	(7)
Order Ref:	SM11
Notes:	Promised to deliver on (8)
	Order arrived four days late
	(9) were missing
Action:	(10) will send missing items today.
	Call customer back today after investigation

c Check your answers by looking at the transcript on page 70.

Reading focus

2 **a** Read the article about transporting goods and then choose the correct title (A–C). Try to predict the missing words as you read.

A Shipping faster than road haulage
B Short-sea shipping gaining popularity
C Better shipping links for Europe

Short-sea shipping is based on the concept of carrying freight door-to-door, or factory to factory, over (1).................... short distances. Given the increase in traffic (2)....................on the roads and the railways' lack of flexibility, short-sea shipping is fast becoming the modern (3)....................to road haulage.

There are many other advantages to short-sea shipping. It is very competitive as costs can be up to 25% cheaper in some cases. It is also flexible, (4).................... more than 300 inland and coastal ports in Europe alone. It offers more (5).................... than road haulage and it has a better environmental track record as (6).................... are lower.

Although short-sea shipping is more reliable, with (7)....................transit times, these may be much longer than for other (8)....................of transport. For example, the transport from Santander (Spain) to Emden (Germany) would take seven days by road, nine by rail and thirteen by sea. (9)...................., transit times may be affected by bad weather in winter. Other (10).................... include potential damage to goods because of the additional handling required and the possibility of delays at ports. Industry experts (11)....................that for short-sea shipping companies to compete more effectively, more service providers are needed, port facilities need to be improved and there should be a total (12).................... to quality and cost management.

b Read the article again. For each gap 1–14, circle the correct answer (A, B, C or D).

1	A equally	B completely	C relatively	D especially
2	A congestion	B obstruction	C overcrowding	D overflow
3	A option	B alternative	C choice	D selection
4	A sailing	B utilising	C manipulating	D dealing
5	A capacity	B room	C space	D dimension
6	A emissions	B fumes	C contaminations	D wastes
7	A confirmed	B certain	C definite	D guaranteed
8	A ways	B methods	C styles	D processes
9	A Furthermore	B Nevertheless	C Consequently	D Understandably
10	A examples	B reasons	C issues	D points
11	A tell	B demonstrate	C see	D say
12	A involvement	B co-operation	C development	D commitment

- Read the whole sentence carefully and look for clues in the sentences before and after each gap.
- When you have finished, read the text through again to check it makes sense.

Follow-up

Did you get any wrong answers?

- In some cases the words have very similar meanings. Getting the right answer depends on:

  <u>A knowledge of collocations</u>
  Number 8: 'methods of transport' is a common collocation. 'means of transport' and 'modes of transport' would also be correct but not 'styles/ways/processes'.

  <u>B knowledge of the correct term</u>
  Number 6: emissions

  <u>C understanding the function of different sentences</u>
  Number 9: This sentence is giving more information about problems with transit times.

- Understanding why the other options are wrong is a good way to build your vocabulary.

Look at your wrong answers and think about why they are wrong.

Writing focus

3 **a** You work for a small furniture manufacturer transporting furniture by road to customers all over Europe. You want some information about other methods of transport. Write an email to your assistant, Andrew Marsh (between 40–50 words):

- explaining why you want this information ← *give a reason: e.g. road haulage company expensive?/unreliable?*
- asking him to write a report on all transport options ← *use language for requests: e.g. Could you ....? I'd be grateful if you could ....*
- saying what type of information he should include. *e.g. cost?/delivery times?/reliability?*

To: Andrew Marsh
Subject: transport report

---

b Look at the model answers on page 79. Which one do you think is better? Why?

/TIP\ Check your work by making sure you have:
- included all the relevant information
- written 40–50 words
- checked for spelling/grammar mistakes
- read your email to make sure it makes sense.

Self-assessment: writing in an appropriate style

4 Which statement is true for you? Put a tick or a cross in the box next to each statement.

☐ I avoid using more complex grammatical structures because I am afraid of making mistakes.

☐ I try to use new business vocabulary where possible.

☐ The letters/emails I write are sometimes too informal for business situations.

☐ Because I translate from my own language, my emails are sometimes too complicated and difficult to understand.

⚠ TIP It's a good idea to try to use a wider range of vocabulary and structures. Look carefully at any business correspondence that you receive from English speakers. Collect useful phrases and expressions from them to use when you are writing.

Speaking focus

5 **a** Look at the prompt card and make some notes.

b Read the mini-presentation. Use the words in the box to complete the gaps.

> WHAT'S IMPORTANT WHEN DEALING WITH COMPLAINTS?
> • Apologising
> • Taking action
> •
> •

a In my opinion	b Another important point
c for example	d That means

> It's very important to apologise to customers when they complain; even if it's not your fault. It's also the best way to stop someone feeling angry. Customer service staff should apologise to customers when they make the complaint and then customers should also receive a written apology after any investigation if the company is at fault.
>
> Taking action is very important because if the customer feels nothing is being done about their problem, next time they will take their business to one of your competitors. (1)................... to remember is that you may lose more than one customer in this situation because dissatisfied customers may damage your reputation by complaining about you to other potential customers. (2)................... companies should have very clear policies and procedures for dealing with complaints so that they are dealt with as efficiently as possible. (3)................... keeping accurate records and checking that appropriate action is being taken. It's very frustrating, (4)..................., for customers to have to keep calling a company and each time speak to a different person and have to explain the problem again and again.

c Listen to the recording and check your answers.

d Look at the prompt card and prepare a mini-presentation. Use some of the phrases from 5b.

e Give a one minute presentation.

> WHAT'S IMPORTANT WHEN A COMPANY RECEIVES A LOT OF COMPLAINTS?
> • Investigation
> • Compensation
> •
> •

12 Reporting

Listening focus

1 a Listen to part of a presentation about the use of mobile technology. For each question circle the correct answer (A, B or C).

1 The survey shows that most companies

A are only making limited use of mobile technology.
B are using mobile technology extensively.
C believe mobile technology is important for the future of their business.

2 A common opinion among staff is that mobile technology

A has made their work easier.
B has increased their workload.
C is essential for their work.

3 What impact has mobile technology had on the majority of companies so far?

A It has changed their marketing strategy.
B It has helped them to reach a wider customer base.
C It has made little difference.

4 The survey shows that smaller companies

A have greater control over their mobile resources.
B invest more heavily in mobile equipment.
C restrict the amount of mobile equipment staff purchase.

5 Having a coordinated plan will mean companies can

A invest more in mobile equipment.
B keep mobile equipment up to date.
C get discounts for large orders of mobile equipment.

6 What is the biggest factor preventing further investment in mobile technology?

A cost
B return on investment
C security concerns

b Listen again and check your answers.

 First listening: Don't worry if you miss an answer; keep going or you will miss the answer to the next question.

Second listening: Check your answers correspond to what is actually said and don't just contain similar words. Remember – the answers are often paraphrases of what is actually said.

Checking your work: Make sure the options you have chosen answer the question.

c Look at the transcript on page 71 and underline the parts that gave you the answers.

Self-assessment: listening to presentations

2 **Which statement is true for you? Put a tick or a cross in the box next to each statement.**

☐ I found listening to the presentation on mobile technology very difficult.

☐ I can understand presentations more easily if there are visuals (graphs/charts etc.).

☐ I can understand presentations if I am familiar with the topic.

☐ I am confident enough to ask questions at the end of presentations.

If you had problems understanding the presentation on mobile technology was this because:

- you didn't know some of the key vocabulary?
- the speaker spoke too fast?
- both?

⚠️ TIP Actively learn vocabulary. Use spidergrams and lists of synonyms to help you remember new words.
Practise listening as much as possible. There are many business reports on cable TV which will help you get used to the speed of English.

Reading focus: summaries

3 **Read the summary below. There are nine extra words which are not needed (they are either grammatically incorrect or do not fit with the sense of the text). Underline the extra words.**

SUMMARY

<u>Presentation on mobile technology use</u>

According to a recent survey, most of companies:

- are only using mobile technology in a limited way
- have noticed no impact on business models
- keep records of how much mobile equipment they are own.

Many companies are prevented from having further investment in mobile technology because of budget restrictions. However, other companies feel the high investment is only worth it because of the guaranteed return on investment.

The survey showed that employees believe the use of mobile technology will increase up slightly. However employees feel improved communications it also mean they will be expected to work faster.

Having a coordinated plan is too important because:

- companies can get more better discounts on purchases of mobile equipment
- money is not been wasted on unnecessary equipment.

Writing focus: reports

 4 You work for a large firm of accountants. Look at the email and survey below on which you have made some handwritten notes. Write a report for your boss, Ed Farel, using all your notes (between 120–140 words).

- Choose an appropriate title.
- Decide which information to include.
- Decide how to organise your report. Headings? Bullet points?

> I am concerned about the rising cost of the company's mobile phone bill. I'd be grateful if you could do an evaluation of managers' use of mobile phones and say whether we need to introduce a new policy.
>
> Thanks
>
> Ed

Say why you think this is a good idea

Survey of managers' mobile phone use

Percentage of mobile phones issued to:

NOTE: explain if this is necessary

■ senior managers	28%
■ middle managers	35%
■ junior managers	37%

Percentage of calls made to:

■ clients	36%
■ colleagues	32%
■ family/friends	32%

NOTE: issue guidelines on personal use

Percentage of international calls made	38%
Percentage of calls made while on business trips	58%

NOTE: say what recommendations to make about these calls

Model answer ▶ page 79

Speaking focus: discussion

5 You work for a large construction firm involved in many projects abroad. The company wants to issue new guidelines on the use of company mobile phones. You have been asked to make some recommendations. Discuss the situation with a partner and decide:

- what kind of guidelines would be appropriate
- how to assess staff needs for mobile phones.

Before you start, think of some ideas, for example:
- Types of phone-calls?
- Possible alternatives?
- How to enforce the new policy?

Try to keep your discussion going for about three minutes.

Model answer ▶ *CD track 48*

13 Presentations

Reading focus: multiple-choice questions

1 **a** **Look at the article below on how to persuade people during presentations.**

Which of the following areas do you think will be mentioned?

- knowing a lot about your audience ☐
- the type of room where the presentation is given ☐
- what to wear ☐
- ways of presenting information ☐
- a bad experience ☐
- having a good knowledge of your product/service ☐
- ways of getting your audience involved ☐

b **Read the article quickly and see if your predictions were correct.**

The art of persuasion

Just before I began the presentation, the project manager of the buying committee told me that the key decision-maker would miss the first 20 minutes of my talk. The whole presentation was scheduled to last about 60 minutes. Thinking on my feet, I changed the order and described the product benefits at the end.

The fact that in this case the manager concerned felt it to be an efficient use of his time to avoid the beginning of the sales presentation tells us a lot about what has happened to the reputation of salespeople and our sales presentations. From past experience he imagined that he would have to sit through yet another PowerPoint presentation showing slide after slide on the company's history, number of employees, etc. So he chose instead to attend only the product demonstration part of the presentation.

We can see from this story that prospective customers are not interested in the size of your factory and the number of employees you have. No-one cares that you have 735 employees until you have proved that you can help resolve one of their business problems. And the way to do that is to get the decision-makers to believe you're not acting in your own self-interest. You've got to convince the customer you're acting in their interest. Very skilful persuaders often seem to act in a way that seems – initially anyhow – contrary to their best interests. For example, they'll tell their audience about a deficiency in one of their products to win them over.

You can influence people in two ways: through their head or through their heart. And while we'd all like to think that the rational side of us is the one we use to make decisions, the fact is that our emotional brain is the one that reacts when we're being persuaded. We make decisions emotionally first and then justify it with reasons afterwards. In other words, when we go out and buy a car, we first fall in love with the look and the feel and the colour and only later does our rational side of the brain convince us that the price is right or it's a good long-term investment.

One way to appeal to an audience's emotions during a presentation is by telling stories. This is also the easiest way to get an audience's attention. Tell a story

c **Underline the parts of the text which describe:**

1 the problem in paragraph 1.
2 the point the writer is making in paragraph 2.
3 how to win the confidence of an audience.
4 what the rational side of our brain does.
5 why the writer thinks stories are an effective presentation tool.
6 the advice the writer gives in the last paragraph.

about one of your customers who had a big problem and how they solved it by doing business with you. Take your feature benefit points and weave them into the story. They will have ten times the impact and will stay in your audience's mind for longer. They will also generate interesting discussions about the customer's business problems and how you can solve them.

It's very tempting when you are short of time to use pre-prepared PowerPoint slides to structure your presentation but it's far more effective to give your audience something more personal and relevant. Relying heavily on PowerPoint slides is not only boring for your audience; it suggests that you lack the confidence to speak to them as individuals. So, what should you do with all those PowerPoint slides that someone in marketing spent hours developing? Print them out as a handout, and give it to your audience at the end of your presentation.

d Read the article again. Look at questions 1–6 and for each question choose the correct answer (A, B, C or D).

1 What problem is described in the first paragraph?

A The key decision-maker did not attend.
B The presentation had to be cut short by 20 minutes.
C The presenter had to make last-minute changes to his presentation.
D The key decision-maker missed an important part of the presentation.

> **TIP** Try to find the answers before you read the options A, B, C or D.

2 The point the writer is making about presentations in the second paragraph is that

A presentations have become too predictable.
B audiences should always stay for the whole presentation.
C the decision-maker was wrong to make assumptions about his presentation.
D the presenter should not use PowerPoint.

3 The best way to win the confidence of an audience is to

A be honest about your product's limitations.
B ask them about their business problems.
C use persuasive sales tactics.
D show you care about their needs.

4 According to the writer, the rational side of our brain

A plays no part in the decision-making process.
B is stronger in some people than others.
C should be used more when we make decisions.
D is used to support the decisions we make emotionally.

5 The writer believes stories are an effective presentation tool because they are

A useful for encouraging audience participation.
B more memorable.
C easy for people to understand.
D interesting.

6 What advice does the writer give in the last paragraph?

A Use slides adapted for your audience at each presentation.
B Avoid using too many PowerPoint slides.
C Have a clear structure to presentations.
D Make sure you give a written summary at the end of the presentation.

2 What do you think is the most useful piece of information in the article?

Language focus

 3 Which of the following verbs can you use in sentences 1–3?

convinced	influenced	suggested
persuaded	advised	recommended

1 My manager .... me to attend the workshop on presentations.
2 The presenter .... my decision to buy his company's product.
3 My boss .... making more eye-contact with the audience.

Self-assessment: reading and multiple-choice tasks

4 Which statement is true for you? Put a tick or a cross in the box next to each statement.

☐ In the multiple-choice reading task I got several wrong answers.

If this was because you didn't understand a lot of the vocabulary, you need to practise trying to guess the meaning of unfamiliar words from the context. Read short articles from newspapers and magazines or business reports all the way through without using a dictionary. Try to guess the meaning of words you don't know and then check using a dictionary.

Or perhaps you didn't read the questions/text carefully enough? Make sure you underline key words/ideas in the text and in the questions.

☐ I got more than half the answers right but it took a long time.

Try to identify quickly the parts that are being tested by underlining the key words. Don't waste time struggling to understand parts that are not tested.

☐ I found it difficult to select the correct option.

Two of the options are wrong, so try to eliminate these quickly. One option may be partly right or it may be right but not actually answer the question. Only one option will (a) answer the question and (b) match the information in the text.

☐ I completed the task without too much difficulty.

Well done!

Writing focus

 5 You work for an organisation that runs one-day presentation training courses for companies. Look at the notes you have written on the comments from colleagues on Billy Dryden's presentation and the notes you have written on the Presentation outline. Write a report for Billy Dryden on his performance using all your handwritten notes (between 120–140 words).

 TIP
- Underline the most important information.
- Decide which information to include in the report.
- Think about the ideas and information you need to provide, e.g. a suggestion on how to avoid looking nervous.

Presenter: Billy

Didn't rely on notes — NOTE: excellent!

Seems very nervous — NOTE: suggest how to avoid looking nervous

---

Presentation Outline

Presenter: Billy Dryden

Introduction: NOTE: Remind Billy why eye-contact is important

Company history — NOTE: too long. Explain why should be shorter

The Future

New opportunities — NOTE: nice slides but too many: explain disadvantage

Possible threats — disadvantage

Conclusion

Aims for the short-term

Model answer ▶ *page 79*

Listening focus

6 a Match phrases A–H with the stages of a presentation 1–8.

A Welcoming the audience
B Giving a summary of the main points
C Complimenting the speaker
D Asking for clarification
E Introducing a new point
F Introducing the speaker
G Responding to a question
H Giving an outline of the presentation

1 I've divided the presentation into three parts.
2 First we looked at ... Second ... And finally we ...
3 I'd like to move on now.
4 Thank you all for coming.
5 You mentioned that ... Could you explain in a little more detail?
6 I think your suggestion for improving ... was excellent.
7 That's a good point. I'm glad you raised that.
8 We're very pleased to welcome ... who has come to tell us about ...

b Listen to five recordings from different presentations. For each recording, decide what the speaker is doing. Choose one stage A–H for each recording. Play the recording twice.

1 .... 2 .... 3 .... 4 .... 5 ....

c Check your answers by reading the transcript on page 72. Underline the phrases which give you the correct answer.

Speaking focus

 7 a Discuss the following questions with a partner.

1 What skills do you need to be a good presenter?
2 Do you think people get more nervous doing presentations in front of colleagues or strangers?
3 Do you think you need to be a good public speaker to get to the top of a company?
4 Do you think asking candidates to prepare a presentation for their job interview is a good idea?

b Listen to James being asked the questions. Summarise his answers.

c Discuss these questions with a partner.

1 Do you get nervous before speaking in public?
2 Do you think people can learn to be good presenters?
3 Do you think it's a good idea to get the audience actively involved during a presentation?
4 Do you think presentations are the best way to sell a product or service?

14 | Companies

Listening focus

 a ⊙ You are going to listen to four people giving information about their company. First, look at the list of topics (A–H) and predict the type of information/vocabulary that may be mentioned.

    A The company's main activities
       what the company produces/sells

    B The company's organisational structure
    C The company's market position
    D The company's future plans
    E The company's corporate values
    F The company's investors
    G The company's recent changes
    H The company's recent achievements

b ⊙ Which topic (A–H) is each speaker talking about?
Listen and write the correct letter next to numbers 1–4.

    1 ....
    2 ....
    3 ....
    4 ....

⚠ TIP If you decide you have chosen one wrong option during the second listening, it may be necessary to change more than one answer.

c Listen again and check your answers.

d Look at the transcript on page 73.

Reading focus

 a Look at the missing sentences (A–G) from an article about Vodafone and tick which sentences 1–6 you think are true.

    A This helps us to think about how emerging wireless technologies could be used to meet people's needs now and in the future.

    B To maintain our position as a world leader we must develop new technology for tomorrow while still providing the best services we can to people today.

    C We will soon expect all of these wireless devices to 'talk' to each other and to become an invisible feature of our extended, connected environment.

    D So Vodafone is developing new service ranges that allow customers to access the services they want, wherever they are, without needing to understand or see the technology that enables them to do so.

    E These define our relationships with all our stakeholders and govern how Vodafone conducts its day-to-day business.

    F They will prefer Vodafone because the experience of using Vodafone will be the best they can find.

    G But at Vodafone we believe this is more than just a fact of geography; it is a source of strength.

1 It is taken from the company's website or brochure. ☐

2 It is from a newspaper. ☐

3 It is about a specific new product. ☐

4 It contains general information about the company. ☐

5 It is about recent developments at Vodafone. ☐

6 It is about Vodafone's plans for the future. ☐

b **Read the article and check your predictions. As you read, think about what kind of information is missing:**

- an example?   - an explanation?   - further detail?   - new information?

Vodafone's vision

Our vision is to be the world's mobile communications leader – helping individuals, businesses and communities be more connected in a mobile world. Our aim is for our customers to use mobile communications to make their lives richer, more fulfilled, more connected. (0)........F................ We will lead in making the mobile the primary means of personal communications for every individual around the world.

Our values guide the way we act. Our values are about how we feel – in other words the passions that make us the company we are. In 2002 we introduced a set of ten business principles to make our vision and values happen. (1)............................ Employees at all levels are expected to act in accordance with the business principles.

With operations worldwide, Vodafone is not only multinational but multicultural. (2)............................ This is because the diversity among our employees is a source of creativity, leadership and innovation. We are building a culture that respects the value of differences among us and encourages individuals to contribute their best within an environment that is inclusive, open, flexible and fair.

Vodafone takes the future very seriously. (3)............................ We do this by offering both **mainstream** mobile products along with the **pioneering** new wireless devices that will become the essential services of tomorrow. We move forward by having one foot in the present and one foot in the future.

One example of this is our role in facilitating people's access to the ever-increasing connectivity, services and information that the Internet has enabled. (4)............................ This is our **core competence** and one that we aim to extend to meet the changing needs of our customers and societies. To make this possible, our forward-looking specialists constantly monitor and evaluate developments and trends in a range of relevant areas, including society, lifestyles and user behaviour.

New developments in science and technology have already had an enormous impact on the way we live and work today. More change is on its way with the development of even smarter, smaller devices with faster wireless connectivity. (5)............................ This could challenge the whole way the industry operates now and we may see new relationships developing between communications providers to deliver **seamless solutions** across a multitude of networks and devices. This is why we look at the complete picture when we plan for the future.

c Read the article again. For each gap 1–5, choose the correct answer A–G.

d Read through the article to check that you have filled each gap with a sentence that both:

- fits the meaning
- fits grammatically.

Language focus

 a Try to guess the meaning of the words in bold from the text.

b Match the phrases to the correct meaning.

| mainstream | pioneering | core competence | seamless solution |

1 ....: normal or established

2 ....: an effective answer to a business problem or issue

3 ....: experimental or new

4 ....: something which a company is known for or skilled in

Writing focus

 a Look at the information below. Your company wants to inform staff about a new funding scheme for training purposes. Managers need to:

- explain what the funding is for
- say what the aim of the scheme is
- say which employees can apply.

b Look at this email. Does it provide all the necessary information?

> We are pleased to announce a new funding scheme for employees.
>
> The aim of this scheme is to provide funding for training.
>
> Employees may apply for funding for training which leads to a business qualification.

c Rewrite the email so that it includes sufficient and relevant details (between 40–50 words).

Model answer ▶ *page 80*

d Your company is introducing an award for the best employee of the year.

Write an email to your team:

- explaining what the aims of the award are
- saying who can enter
- saying what the prize is.

Model answer ▶ *page 80*

Speaking focus

 5 **a** **You are going to prepare a mini-presentation on business principles. Look at the prompt card and the questions below.**

Which of the following do you think it would be appropriate to talk about?

- the size of the company
- how the company wants to treat its customers
- the company's main strengths
- its attitude to the environment
- how the company is structured
- how the company plans to achieve its aims
- its policy on training staff
- its employment policy
- where the company sees itself in five years

Which are values and which are part of a company's vision?

Can you think of any other principles?

Why is it important for a company to have these principles?

b **Give a one minute presentation. Practise doing your presentation two or three times.**
Model answer ▶▶ *CD track 59*

> **WHAT'S IMPORTANT WHEN ...?**
> Describing a company's business principles:
> - values
> - vision
> -
> -

Self-assessment: pronunciation

6 **Record yourself doing the mini-presentation again or ask a partner/teacher to help assess your pronunciation. Which statement is true for you? Put a tick or a cross in the box next to each statement.**

☐ My pronunciation is clear but very slow.

Having clear pronunciation is very important, but remember, in English not all words are stressed equally. Practise listening to the words which aren't stressed in a sentence and pay attention to the rhythm of English.

☐ I think it's difficult to understand my pronunciation because I speak too quickly.

Fluency is great but not if people can't understand you. Slow down and focus on accurate pronunciation.

☐ My accent is very strong and some sounds are not clear.

Ask your teacher to recommend some pronunciation workbooks such as *English Pronunciation in Use* by Mark Hancock.

☐ To make my pronunciation better I need to work on intonation and sentence stress.

Listen to yourself giving your presentation and decide which words should be stressed and where your intonation should rise/fall. Practise doing the presentation again and ask a partner/teacher for feedback.

15 Changes at work

Reading focus

 a **Below is an article about why mergers and acquisitions sometimes fail.**

Which of the following do you think are the main reasons for failure?

- poor management
- low staff morale
- high cost of acquisitions
- lack of proper planning
- clash of corporate cultures
- bad timing

b **Read the article and check your answers.**

Why mergers and acquisitions fail

Sometimes the failure of an acquisition to produce good returns for the parent company may be explained by the simple fact that they paid too much for it. (1)............................ the buyer may find that the premium they paid for the acquired company's shares cancels out any (2)........................... made from the acquisition. Even if a deal is financially sound, it may (3)........................... to be a disaster if it is carried out in a way that does not (4)........................... sensitively with the companies' employees and their different corporate cultures. There may be (5)........................... differences between the attitudes and values of the two companies, especially if the new partnership crosses national boundaries (in which case there may also be language (6)........................... to cope with).

A merger or acquisition is an extremely stressful (7)........................... to go through for all concerned: job losses, restructuring, and the (8)........................... of another corporate culture and identity can (9)........................... uncertainty, anxiety and resentment among a company's employees. Research shows that a firm's productivity can (10)........................... by between 25 and 50 per cent while experiencing such a large-scale change and low morale among the workforce is a (11)........................... reason for this. Companies often pay too much attention to the short-term legal and financial issues (12)........................... in a merger or acquisition, and neglect the implications for corporate identity and communication, factors that may prove equally important in the long run because of their (13)........................... on workers' morale and productivity. Managers, who find their authority and promotion (14)........................... suddenly taken away, can be particularly bitter; one survey found that nearly 50 per cent of executives in acquired firms (15)........................... other jobs within one year.

c Read the article again. For each gap 1–15, circle the correct answer (A, B, C or D).

 TIP Remember you need to choose words which fit grammatically as well as having the correct meaning. This means paying attention to collocations and watching out for prepositions.

	A	B	C	D
1	In order to	A consequence	As a result	In spite of
2	interests	gains	investments	advantages
3	find	end	result	prove
4	deal	consider	handle	co-operate
5	high	strong	heavy	hard
6	borders	limits	barriers	restrictions
7	action	process	progress	policy
8	start	opening	launch	introduction
9	create	make	have	start
10	lose	reduce	drop	cut
11	major	great	deep	sharp
12	connected	involved	contained	committed
13	effect	result	significance	importance
14	options	prospects	promises	proposals
15	search	apply	change	find

Listening focus

2 a ◉ Listen to part of a presentation reporting on the findings of a survey into company reorganisations. For questions 1–7 circle the correct answer (A, B or C).

TIP
- Before you listen, read the questions (but not the options A–C). This will help you to focus on the information you need to listen for.
- Remember you need to process information – don't just pick an option because it contains the same words as on the recording.

1 According to the survey, business leaders believe company reorganisations

  A are required more frequently than in the past.
  B should be undertaken every three years.
  C are an on-going process.

2 The most common reason given for reorganising was

  A being taken over by another company.
  B the appointment of a new CEO.
  C a decrease in profits

3 Which is considered the most important aim of reorganisation?

  A improved efficiency
  B improved internal effectiveness
  C improved external effectiveness

4 The survey shows that reorganisations

  A achieve all their aims in more than 50% of companies.
  B sometimes result in unexpected improvements.
  C to improve internal effectiveness are the most successful.

5 In future, senior managers will be more influenced by

  A their own teams.
  B consultants' advice.
  C competitors' experiences.

6 What are the findings on the effects of reorganisation on redundancies?

    A Most companies report more than 50% redundancies.
    B Redundancies can lead to improvements in efficiency.
    C Most respondents felt redundancies were not always necessary.

7 Involving employees in decisions about the reorganisation

    A happens in the majority of companies.
    B is considered too time-consuming.
    C leads to improved performance.

c Listen again. Then check your answers by reading the transcript on pages 73 and 74.

Writing focus: reports

 a Your company introduced flexible working in 2002. You have been asked to write a report describing the successes and failures of flexible working. Look at the information below on which you have already made some handwritten notes.

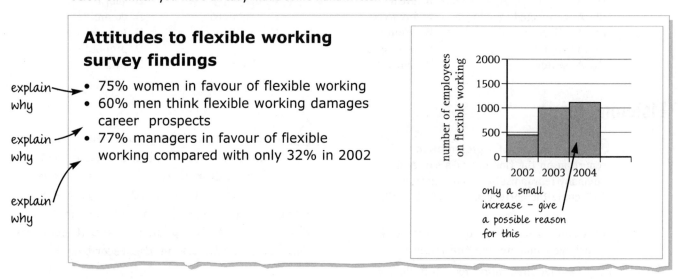

Attitudes to flexible working survey findings

explain why →
- 75% women in favour of flexible working
- 60% men think flexible working damages career prospects

explain why →
- 77% managers in favour of flexible working compared with only 32% in 2002

explain why

only a small increase – give a possible reason for this

b Plan your report.

1 Think about the focus of the report. In this case it is to report on the success/failures of flexible working. Organise the information into two columns.

2 Look at the handwritten notes. Think of a possible reason for each of the notes.

Success/Failure	Reason
75% of women are in	Women with young
favour of flexible working.	children prefer flexible
	working as it allows
	them to spend more time
	with their children.

3 Choose appropriate headings for your report and organise your points under each heading. Remember to include a title.

c Write a first draft of your report (between 120–140 words).

d Ask a teacher for feedback or compare reports with a partner. Then write a final draft of your report.

e *Model answer* ▶ *page 80*

 • Include all the information required
• Organise the information clearly into paragraphs under headings
• Write in an appropriate business style
• Avoid repeating the same words/structures too often
• Check for grammar/spelling mistakes
• Write the correct number of words

Self-assessment: writing reports

 Which statement is true for you? Put a tick or a cross in the box next to each statement.

☐ I find it difficult to know what to write.

It's a good idea to spend time planning with a partner. You can brainstorm ideas together, write your reports separately and then compare them. After this you could write a final draft using the best ideas/language from both your first drafts.

Reading reports on surveys in business magazines will also help with ideas.

☐ I still make too many grammar mistakes.

Always write a first draft, edit it carefully with the help of a teacher/partner and then write a final version.

☐ My range of structure and vocabulary is very basic.

Practise reading newspaper/magazine reports about different types of companies. This will help to develop the range of business words and expressions that you need.

Speaking focus: discussions

 a ⊙ Listen to two colleagues talking about whether a company should introduce flexible working.

What language do Clare and Nick use when they disagree with each other?

b Following a recent merger, the company you work for is relocating to new offices in a cheaper area, 250 km away and you have been asked to help plan the move. Discuss the situation with a partner and decide:

• what information staff will need to know about the relocation
• what practical help the company should give.

⚠️TIP Disagreeing politely
• Don't you think that ...?
• Sorry but I'm not sure I agree.
• I'm not sure about that.
• I see what you mean, but ...

Transcripts

Unit 1

Listening focus 1

2a

WOMAN: Salmon Partners. Sarah Myers speaking.
MAN: Oh hello. Could I speak to Oliver Richardson please?
WOMAN: I'm afraid he's not at his desk. Can I ask who's calling?

Listening focus 2

3a

1

WOMAN: Salmon Partners. Sarah Myers speaking.
MAN: Oh hello. Could I speak to Oliver Richardson please?
WOMAN: I'm afraid he's not at his desk. Can I ask who's calling?
MAN: My name's Martin Donoghue. That's D O N O G H U E. I'm the new events manager at the Book Centre.
WOMAN: Oh yes?
MAN: Well. I was just calling to introduce myself and to give Mr Richardson some information about next month's trade show which I think he'll find very useful.
WOMAN: I see. Well if I can take your phone number I'll pass your message on to Mr Richardson.
MAN: Fine. It's 014432 349876.
WOMAN: Thanks for your call.

2

RECEPTIONIST: Vikram Supplies. Good morning.
FRANK: Oh hello. Could you put me through to Chris Parnell please?
RECEPTIONIST: I'll try her number for you.
SHONA: Sales Department. Shona Birt speaking. Can I help you?
FRANK: I'm trying to contact Chris Parnell.
SHONA: I'm afraid she's in a meeting. Can I ask who's calling?
FRANK: It's Frank North from Klines.
SHONA: Sorry can you spell the name of the company?
FRANK: K L I N E S.
SHONA: Thank you.
FRANK: I've arranged a meeting with Chris for the 12th but if possible I'd like to make it later that week; the 16th would suit me best.
SHONA: Any time that day?
FRANK: I've got another appointment in Sheldon at ten thirty so the earliest I could get there would be half past twelve if that's OK with Chris.
SHONA: She should be out of her meeting at quarter past eleven so I'll get her to call you then. Can I take your number?
FRANK: Yes. It's 07721 337065 or she can try the mobile which is 00466 2121378.
SHONA: OK. Thanks for calling.
FRANK: Thanks for your help. Bye.

Speaking focus

6b

Obviously it's important to try and achieve your aims when you're cold calling. It probably helps to have clear aims in mind for each call. For example, getting the name of the right person to speak to from one company or to arrange a meeting. But I think you can use every call to find out more about potential customers; who the decision makers are, how interested they are, how big the company is and so on. So you shouldn't feel worried if you don't always achieve your main aims.

It's a good idea to prepare what you want to say before you call so that you don't forget anything important. However, you shouldn't prepare too well – it's important to sound natural on the telephone and not like you're reading from a script.

Unit 2

Listening focus

6b

1

Well, I'm sure everyone here found that was very useful and on behalf of the committee I'd like to say we really appreciate the fact that you've given up your time to be here today. We're very grateful for all the advice that you've given us and it's been a wonderful opportunity for us to find out more about your organisation. Now Mr Bowman has kindly agreed to take any questions so if you ....

2

I'm sorry I haven't got back to you about the meeting until now but we've been very busy with another project. Anyway, I'm calling to confirm the meeting on the 25th. Could, you let me know if you are still free? I'd be grateful if you could get back to me as soon as possible as I need to confirm the date with everyone involved. Thanks very much.

3

I just wanted to let you know that the management team have now had a chance to look at all the options and after careful consideration we've decided to go with another agency. I know that you and your team have put a lot of work into this and I'd like to thank you personally for your efforts but in this instance I regret we won't be able to take your offer any further.

4

I'm afraid the panel haven't reached agreement yet and so I'm not in a position to tell you at the moment whether your application has been successful. I'll have to check when they're planning to make the announcement and get back to you. Sorry I can't be more helpful. Thank you very much for calling.

Speaking focus

7a

INTERVIEWER: How much do you use email at work?

MANAGER: Well I actually use email all the time for work. I ... erm ... I usually get about ... about 50 emails a day and I'm not sure exactly but I suppose I send around 25 a day.

INTERVIEWER: What advantages do you think there are for employees in using emails rather than letters?

MANAGER: Well, er ... the main, the main advantage is that it saves time and it's more convenient. I mean, it takes two days to send a letter, four or five days to send a letter abroad or, or sometimes more. Yes, so the main advantage is that it saves time. It's, it's also cheaper than sending a letter.

INTERVIEWER: But do you think email has changed the way people work?

MANAGER: It's hard to remember what it was like before! Erm, I know that when the network is down in my office we all feel quite lost and er, cut off. Anyway, I think we're all erm, well very dependent on email now.

INTERVIEWER: Do you think there are any problems for companies using email?

MANAGER: I think the main problem is security. We have er, very, very strict guidelines in our office about the kind of information we can send by email. Er, we're not supposed to send attachments of confidential information, for example. Also, you, you have to be very careful because emails cannot be deleted; they're a permanent record and I know some companies have had emails used as evidence against them in court cases.

INTERVIEWER: Have you experienced any problems using email?

MANAGER: Erm ... my main problem with email is that I get, er, far too many. I, I said before that emails save time but really a lot of my time is wasted reading unnecessary emails or erm, or being sent multiple copies of the same information. It can be very frustrating because instead of getting on with your job you have to, to deal with all this correspondence.

INTERVIEWER: Do you think companies should try to control the number of internal emails that are sent?

MANAGER: I think that limiting the amount of email sent internally would help. It er, well, it would cut my inbox by half at least and the other thing is, it might encourage people to talk to each other more.

Unit 3

Listening focus

3a

MAN: What do you think makes your team leader successful? Camilla?

CAMILLA: Well, probably the best thing about working for John is that it's more of a partnership. He always wants to know what people on the team think and he's always prepared to listen to advice before he makes a decision.

SARA: Yeah that's true. He makes you feel valued. And he's not one of these managers that delegates everything to other people.

CAMILLA: No. He works really hard.

MAN: OK. I wonder if one reason why the team works well together is because you're all quite similar.

SARA: I'm not sure about that. It's hard to know how similar we are. I mean we're all doing similar jobs and we're a similar age but we don't spend a lot of time together.

CAMILLA: Mmm and it's good we don't always share the same opinions. It makes the team more creative – you can always rely on someone to come up with a brilliant solution to a problem.

MAN: That's interesting. Have you noticed any disadvantages to working in a virtual team?

CAMILLA: I don't think so. Not really. I generally enjoy it. It gives my work a different focus and I think we get a lot more done. Do you agree, Sara?

SARA: I suppose so, but it can be difficult to find out what's happening if you miss a meeting. You can waste a lot of time chasing people for information.

CAMILLA: Oh I don't think so. I think people are pretty good at communicating.

MAN: It would be interesting to see what the other people in the team think about that but let's talk about any changes you've noticed in the way the team works recently.

CAMILLA: Um. Not so much recently, no. When the team was formed our targets kept changing. But in the last six months it's settled and I think now we all understand what we're trying to achieve.

SARA: Yes. Before it was difficult to achieve anything because different people kept joining and leaving the team. Now it's easier and we don't need to have so many meetings.

MAN: Is there anything you'd like to change?

SARA: Um. Well recently we've had new equipment installed but I think we need some time to learn how to use it properly. What do you think Camilla?

CAMILLA: Yes I think that's very important. And if we did a workshop with the whole team we would also have a chance to spend some time face to face.

SARA: Mmm, that's a good point. I think we should suggest doing that.

MAN: Great. Thanks for all the information. It's been very helpful.

Speaking focus

5c

MAN: How useful do you think it would be to have more face-to-face meetings?

WOMAN: I don't think that would help at all. I think a lot of time is wasted in meetings especially if there's no clear purpose.

MAN: What about having monthly briefing meetings – you know just to keep other people informed about new developments or any problems?

WOMAN: I suppose so but they would have to be managed very carefully. There's no point in having meetings unless there's a real need for it. We could try it for a few months and then review it.

MAN: OK. So that's one thing we could recommend. Right ... more social events?

WOMAN: I'm not sure that would work. People don't like giving up their free time for work unless it's for something really special. And it could be expensive if we organise exciting events that people would really want to come to.

MAN: Yes, that's a good point. But social events don't have to be big or involve a lot of expense. I wonder if trying to encourage senior managers to have lunch in the canteen with some of the junior staff might help.

WOMAN: Mmm. That's worth a try. Or just inviting people for informal drinks in the bar after work.

MAN: Good idea.

Unit 4

Listening focus

7a

1

OK. So we're all agreed that Josep is by far the stronger candidate and that we'd like to offer him the post. We know that he's really interested in the job. The only problem is that he's clearly not satisfied with the package we're offering. What we need to do now is discuss how much more we're prepared to offer him and what we think it will take to get him to accept.

2

I just felt it was time to move on. The company had quite a rigid career structure and I realised that I'd have more opportunities to develop my skills if I took a job abroad. I don't regret that at all. I really learnt a lot while I was out there and was given much more responsibility than in my old job.

3

I'm a little concerned about your lack of line management experience. As you know the post involves line managing a team of project officers located on different sites. What I'd like to know is how well you think your previous experience has prepared you for taking on this role and what skills you think you may need to develop in order to succeed in this role.

4

I'd like to invite Stella for a second interview. I know she doesn't have as much relevant experience as some of the other candidates but I think she has a lot to offer and I was very impressed with the way she performed in the first interview. I don't know if everyone feels the same way but I think the company should consider employing someone from a different industry who has a fresh approach.

Speaking focus

8c

Asking questions is important because it's your opportunity to find out more about the company. It's important to find out about pay and conditions if these have not been mentioned because without this kind of information you can't make an informed decision about whether you want to join the company. Sometimes interviewers want to see if candidates can take the initiative and ask searching questions.

It's also important to ask questions during the interview to show you're interested and that you have thought about the job seriously.

It's very difficult to think about your body language when you are nervous but at least you should try to make eye contact with each of the interviewers and to sit still, so that you look calm and confident.

If you have to do a presentation as part of the interview you should practise a lot and get a friend to watch your body language; how you stand, what you do with your hands. So you can learn to look confident.

Unit 5

Listening focus

1a

1

LESLIE: Erm, Mark. Could I have a word?

MARK: Yes, what is it Leslie?

LESLIE: Well I've got a problem with one of my shifts and I was wondering if I could change it.

MARK: Which day is it?

LESLIE: Monday.

MARK: Right. That's the 25th. So could you work the 26th instead?

LESLIE: I've got to take my father for a check-up at the hospital that day, so it would have to be the 27th. I've found someone who doesn't mind swapping with me.

MARK: OK. Hang on. Which shift are you going to work that day?

LESLIE: It's the early shift. If I was working the later shift on the 25th, I wouldn't have a problem. But my sister arrives very early that day from Canada. I really want to meet her from the airport because I haven't seen her for two years.

MARK: I see. You said you'd found someone who is willing to swap shifts with you?

LESLIE: Yeah. Anna'll do it.

MARK: Which Anna is that? Anna Richards?

LESLIE: Sorry. No. Anna Black. She started last month.

MARK: Oh yes. Well, that should be fine. Thanks for letting me know.

LESLIE: Thank you very much.

2

MAN: So have you decided which training course to organise?

WOMAN: Well, I was wondering if it would be possible to do a two-day course at the Calford training centre. The programme looks really good and I think staff would really benefit.

MAN: Mmm. They're very expensive. Isn't there another course available?

WOMAN: Calford only do a two-day programme but the City Training Centre do a one-day workshop ...

MAN: They're quite good. We've used them a few times before. Their courses are certainly much cheaper.

WOMAN: Let's see ... this is it. It's called 'Easy delegating'.

MAN: It looks interesting. Is that held at their training centre?

WOMAN: It says they can do it there or in our office.

MAN: It'd be better to do it here. To cut costs a bit.

WOMAN: Yes. Do you think I can go ahead and book that then?

MAN: I suppose so. Can I just make a note of the cost before you go?

WOMAN: It'll be £80 per day per participant and there'll be six of us – so it'll come to £480 and that includes a free follow-up training pack and all meals.

MAN: When are you going to book it for?

WOMAN: Things will be fairly quiet the week of the 19th. So would the 21st be OK?

MAN: Yes, but try to make sure everyone does attend – we don't want to have to organise another course.

WOMAN: Yes, of course.

1 Follow-up

1 I was wondering if I could have a word with you.
2 Would it be OK if I joined you at eleven?
3 Would it be possible for you to finish the report by Friday?
4 Is it OK if I let you know tomorrow?
5 Do you think you could check these figures for me?

Speaking focus

5 Model answer

I think providing clear instructions is absolutely essential. Managers who delegate without doing this are probably not going to get satisfactory results. It's also very important to be specific about what you want and how you want it done and to make sure everyone knows what's expected. It's a good idea to provide instructions in writing. I think this is a good practice to follow even if you're dealing with experienced staff who've done similar tasks in the past because then staff don't have the excuse of saying they didn't realise they were supposed to do something.

Monitoring is equally important for larger projects. Staff should be asked to report progress on a regular basis and to provide evidence that the work is being done. This gives everyone the opportunity to discuss any problems and to sort them out before it's too late. If you wait until the deadline to do this then a lot of time can be wasted. And the whole point of delegating is to save managers' time.

Unit 6

Listening focus

1a

1

I'm not sure exactly what you mean by that. Do you think you could be a bit more specific? I mean I understand what the problem is but I'm not sure I understand how you want me to solve it. Perhaps it would be a bit clearer if you could show me some examples of other teams' work.

2

That's a fair point although I don't entirely agree with everything that's been said. However, I'm prepared to admit that some of the responsibility for this problem lies in the way the project was set up in the first place. And I do accept that my team are at least partly to blame for the lack of communication.

3

Well, I think you should be quite satisfied with the way things are going. You've really made a lot of progress over the last three months and certainly I would say that the best thing for you now would be to gain some overseas experience. Perhaps you could spend six months in one of our Asian offices. That way I think you would learn a lot about the markets there.

4

I am well aware that my department have not been performing as well as expected but I'm not sure we're entirely to blame for that. We've been operating in a very competitive market which has made it very difficult to reach our targets. Also, the recent staff cuts have certainly affected our ability to react quickly to new developments.

Speaking focus

6c

WOMAN: So, what do you think the advantages of a reward scheme are for the company?

MAN: Well, it's a good way to motivate employees. If they can see that their hard work will be recognised and rewarded, then they're more likely to work harder and try to achieve more for the company.

WOMAN: Yes. So the company becomes more productive. I think that lots of companies that have tried this have found that staff turnover is reduced.

MAN: Right. Because people feel they are valued ... OK. What kind of rewards do you think we should offer?

WOMAN: I think that people always prefer money. I'm not sure that everyone is interested in gifts or holidays.

MAN: Mmm. The problem with those is that people don't always like the same gifts or want to go to the same places on holiday. But I'm not sure about giving money as a reward because unless it's a lot of money it's not going to make much difference. And the other problem with money is that it just gets added to people's pay packets so there's no opportunity for having a presentation.

WOMAN: What do you mean exactly?

MAN: Well, I think getting recognition for your achievements from colleagues is just as important as the reward itself. So I think there needs to be some sort of presentation ceremony – not necessarily something very formal – for the manager to say thank you to employees who have performed well.

WOMAN: Yes, that's a good point. Well what about giving vouchers that can be used in lots of different shops? That way you can have a presentation and the employee gets to choose what they really want.

MAN: That's a good idea. OK. Now we have to decide how to make this popular with employees. Do you have any ideas?

WOMAN: I think that reward schemes often fail because employees think they're not fair. I mean sometimes they see the same colleagues getting rewarded all the time or else the targets are set too high and no-one gets rewarded. In these cases reward schemes de-motivate rather than motivate.

MAN: So the scheme has to be fair to all employees. That means everyone should have the chance of getting a reward which means setting achievable targets.

WOMAN: Exactly. And I also think it really helps if the whole process is transparent so that employees really understand how to achieve the targets.

Unit 7

Listening focus

4a

1

Unocom are planning to invest up to £85m over this and the next financial year in Mushroom, the broadband internet service it bought in May. This news prompted a small rise in shares, which have been gradually recovering after the slump last year. The company said it hoped this new direction would help Mushroom achieve sales of £250m within four years.

2

Two years ago, we lost over 2 million internet members, though this situation has stabilised over the last six months. Part of the problem has been that the market has become far more competitive and for the first time customers have been offered a choice of providers, so really it has been difficult for us to hold onto market share when new competitors are charging less for the basic service.

3

A recent survey of 2,000 web-using Britons showed a whopping 94% had bought something online. This compares to just 37% five years ago. Half of those interviewed believed that 40% or more of their purchases would be done online in five years' time. The research also reveals that many consumers are surprised how easy online shopping is.

4

Some of the smaller operators such as Zac and Molton offer shorter contracts which might appeal to people unwilling to commit to a year's worth of broadband. There is also a huge variety in the amount of features available. Some operators offer webspace, email accounts and free technical support, while others charge extra for these.

Speaking focus

5a

MAN: How do you use the Internet for work purposes?

WOMAN: I use it all the time; mainly for researching competitors and finding out about developments in different markets. The Internet makes it really easy for me to keep up to date with what's going on. It's an amazingly effective research tool.

MAN: How do you think the Internet has changed the way people work?

WOMAN: Although the Internet's made everything faster, it doesn't mean that people have less work to do. People haven't benefited that much because we're just expected to do a lot more than we used to. But certainly we couldn't live without it now. We're becoming more and more dependent on the Internet for all kinds of business activities from sourcing raw materials to selling products.

MAN: What advantages do you think the Internet has brought to smaller companies?

WOMAN: I think the Internet's brought more advantages to smaller companies than any other group. Having a website means a small company can stay 'open' 24 hours a day and reach a much wider market. Thousands of new businesses have started which couldn't have functioned without the Internet.

MAN: Are there any disadvantages for customers in using the Internet?

WOMAN: There are always going to be issues concerning fraud, privacy and security. Many customers are worried about giving personal details such as credit card numbers and there have been lots of cases where people have bought things from companies that don't exist. I think that it's hard to control and that dishonest people will always find a way to abuse the Internet.

Unit 8

Listening focus

1a

1

GEOFF: Hi Sarah. I just wanted to check that you were able to come to the marketing review meeting.

SARAH: It's the 21st isn't it? Oh no, it's the 23rd. The policy meeting is on the 21st. Yes, that's OK. What time will it start?

GEOFF: 10 o'clock I think. That'll give us plenty of time. You know we're in the boardroom, don't you? The conference room was already booked.

SARAH: I'll make a note of that. By the way, is it too late to add something to the agenda?

GEOFF: No.

SARAH: I'd like to say something about new competitors. There are some important issues I think we need to look at.

GEOFF: OK. I'll make sure it's included.

SARAH: Thanks Geoff. Oh, before I forget ... Helen Spencer won't be able to make it. I've asked her to visit the Harlow factory that day.

GEOFF: That's OK. Thanks for letting me know.

2

MARIO: Cristina, it's Mario.

CRISTINA: Oh, hi Mario. What can I do for you?

MARIO: Well, I just wanted to let you know the Credit Control Management Meeting has been brought forward to the 19th.

CRISTINA: Oh right. It's at the same time, is it?

MARIO: Yes. We've got the meeting room booked from 11 to 1.30.

CRISTINA: Fine.

MARIO: Unfortunately Thomas won't be able to chair the meeting as usual because he's on leave that week so Ann Simpson will take his place. We just couldn't find an alternative date when everyone was available.

CRISTINA: Mmm.

MARIO: I know she doesn't know anything about electronic invoicing so it would be useful if you could talk to her about it before the meeting.

CRISTINA: Yes of course. That's no problem.

MARIO: Is there any information she should look at before the meeting?

CRISTINA: The consultant's report is probably the most useful document to look at – I'll make sure she gets sent a copy.

MARIO: Good. Thanks Cristina.

Speaking focus

5 Model answer

MAN: OK. What do you think we need to do to make meetings more effective?

WOMAN: Well, it seems the main problem is that meetings go on too long and don't achieve enough. So I think the first thing we need to do is to make sure meetings stick to scheduled times.

MAN: What do you mean 'scheduled times'?

WOMAN: OK. Each meeting should have a starting and finishing time and also each item on the agenda should have a time limit.

MAN: What happens if you go over the time limit? I mean it's not always possible to predict how long something's going to take.

WOMAN: No. Then it's up to the chair to make a judgement about what to do. But I would say if something is taking longer than anticipated then it needs to be discussed in another meeting.

MAN: That seems sensible. All right. Now I also think it's important to make sure meetings achieve what they are supposed to achieve. The agenda needs to set clearly identifiable aims. If you have a good agenda then the meeting should run according to plan. But the problem is that most chairs don't stick to the agenda and that's when things start to go wrong.

WOMAN: So how can we make sure that staff do these things to make meetings more effective?

MAN: I don't know exactly but in my experience no-one is ever trained how to be a chair. Meetings also tend to be informal which makes it difficult for the person who's supposed to be managing the meeting to take on a formal role as chair. Everyone just speaks when they want to.

WOMAN: Yes. That's an interesting point. So perhaps what we need to do is issue some guidelines on behaviour in meetings.

MAN: But I don't think that will change anything. It needs to be more dynamic. Maybe some training activities involving roleplays. It's more fun and it helps people to remember more easily

WOMAN: Good idea. Basically we need to find ways to make sure everyone understands the rules and is more disciplined in meetings.

MAN: I agree.

Unit 9
Speaking focus

5b

MAN: Do you try to plan your work schedule in advance?

WOMAN: Yes. I usually make a rough monthly plan and then I review it weekly. I make a list of things I have to do in my diary for each week and I tick them off as I get through each task. The only problem with this system is that I often underestimate how much time something is going to take and so the work can build up as more things get added to my to-do list each week.

MAN: How useful do you think it is for companies to organise time management training for their staff?

WOMAN: I'm not sure as I've never been on a time management course. I imagine that a lot of it is common sense and I suppose it depends on how organised you are already. Maybe for some people it really is necessary because they really don't know how to manage their time. I'd be interested to go on one of these courses to see if I could learn anything but generally I think I'm fairly well-organised.

MAN: Do you think people work more effectively when they have to meet a deadline?

WOMAN: Yes, I think having a deadline is essential so you can plan your work. Most people work on several different tasks at the same time and if you don't have deadlines you can't prioritise your tasks.

MAN: How important do you think it is for companies to make sure staff have a good work-life balance?

WOMAN: I think it's really important. I don't think people should be expected to give up their whole lives for their job. And I think companies benefit from helping staff to achieve a better work-life balance because if staff are happier, they're less likely to be stressed, and will take less time off work and change jobs less often.

Listening focus

6a

ADVISOR: So how's it going? Are you finding it any easier to manage your time?

PETER: Yes. The strategies we discussed last time have made a difference. The only problem is that I've been travelling so much lately that it's been difficult to get things done.

ADVISOR: I see. Well perhaps I can help you there. First, are all these business trips really necessary? You know recent studies have shown that 50% of business travellers believe their trips weren't really necessary and that at least a day is wasted each time they travel.

PETER: I can believe it. But it's not that easy to decide whether a trip is worth making. I mean often you don't know until you get there whether it's going to be a waste of time.

ADVISOR: That's true. But each time you're planning a trip the important thing to ask yourself is 'What am I going to get out of this?' If you're going to travel 3,000 miles either to make a presentation to a hundred people or to meet just one person, it's only worth it if this will develop long term relationships.

PETER: I can see that. But what if I decide that all my trips are important? I'm still going to get behind because of all the wasted time sitting in airports and being entertained in the evenings.

ADVISOR: That brings me to my second point. You should be able to use the time you spend away from the office more productively. I mean even if you aim to increase your productivity while actually travelling by only 5%, it would make hours of otherwise 'dead' time purposeful.

PETER: You mean reading reports and looking at emails? I always think I'm going to do that kind of thing when I'm sitting in the airport lounge and during flights but I never do.

ADVISOR: If you use your travelling time more productively, you'll add at least another two hours to your day.

PETER: That's true. I find all the waiting around very frustrating. If I use that time for doing something useful, I might not mind so much. And then when I'm being entertained in the evenings, I can relax, knowing that I've done some work earlier.

ADVISOR: Absolutely.

PETER: Another big problem is catching up with larger projects after I've been away. For example, you know I've been asked to draft the plans for re-organising the department?

ADVISOR: Yes.

PETER: I just can't see how I'm going to get it done because I've got several more trips in the next few weeks.

ADVISOR: Right. Well, the thing to do is to divide it into smaller tasks. Don't try to do it all at once and don't put it off until you get back to the office. If you break it into tasks you can do in 30 minutes, you can do some of them as you travel. You can also delegate these smaller tasks to your staff to do while you're away.

PETER: That might be OK for some tasks but for complex tasks I might spend too much time planning work when I could be actually doing it.

ADVISOR: Well. You can only try it and see. We can talk about it next time. Shall we move on …

Unit 10

Listening focus

5a

1
I'm not sure we can afford to launch our new services in exactly the same way as we did before. The TV campaign was good for raising awareness of the brand and creating the right image but it was very costly and I'm not convinced the return on investment was worth it. I'd be happy to cut it out altogether and explore other alternatives.

2
Questionnaires all ask consumers the same questions and don't ask for enough detail. And trying to get focus groups to tell you what they think of your product or your new brand name doesn't give a true picture of what consumers really think because discussions always get dominated by the strongest character there. You're more likely to succeed if you trust your own instincts and have confidence in your brand.

3
Obviously if you come up with a genuinely new product then it's going to need its own identity and shouldn't be packaged along with any other existing brands. But brand managers these days have a difficult task finding a word that isn't being used by anyone else and also isn't offensive in any language; so what they tend to do now is look for a word that isn't directly associated with what a product or service does but creates an image that's connected with a benefit.

4
I think the message we're trying to get across to consumers in this campaign is quite simple. The first point we need to stress is that we care about quality and we care about good design. Of course we want our customers to feel stylish when they use our products but above all we must stress their reliability. The other thing we want to make clear is that although our products are affordable, they're not cheap. In other words they offer good value for money.

Speaking focus

6c

The first thing to consider when choosing a brand name is the image you want to create. Do you want a name that suggests your product is high-class, sleek and sophisticated or one that suggests it's innovative and exciting? You also have to have a clear idea about what the name can do for the product and what impact you want it to have on potential customers. Do you want to surprise them or make them feel relaxed?

You should research the name carefully to make sure no-one else is using it and you need to find out if the name will travel well. You don't want to end up with a name that means something completely different in another language. A lot of companies use focus groups to try out new names but it's hard for consumers to say whether they like a name if they don't know much about the product and they haven't seen the logo or packaging.

It's very important to get your name trademarked so that the name legally belongs to your company. Then no-one else is allowed to use it. Sometimes you may find that the name is already being used and this means holding up the whole project until another name is chosen.

7b

1 potential, consumer, important, researcher
2 innovative
3 affordable, compatible, reliable
4 comprehensive
5 sophisticated

Unit 11

Listening focus

1a

1 It was ordered on the 13th of March.
2 The account number is B, that's B for Boy, Z 38125.
3 The large tables are 3 m 45 cm long.
4 The average shipment cost for a standard package from London to Paris is £855.90 plus VAT.
5 The cars retail at 25,995.

1b

1

WOMAN: Hello. I'd like to place an order please.

MAN: Of course. Could I have your company name and account number please?

WOMAN: Yes. It's Simpson's. The account number is 0093BJ.

MAN: Is that P for Peter?

WOMAN: No. B for Boy.

MAN: Right I've got your details now. Could you just confirm your company's address for me?

WOMAN: Yes. It's Black's Furniture Warehouse, Unit 13b, Lowick LW5 6PQ.

MAN: Thank you. Is it for kitchen units?

WOMAN: Yes. We'd like some more Riviera kitchen units, in white this time.

MAN: Let's see. That's Reference number CL331. Right ... Yes. We have those in stock. Which size do you want? They come in two sizes.

WOMAN: It's the 870mm by 600mm we need. About ten of those if you've got them in stock. We still have enough of the 720 by 500.

MAN: So that's ten 870 by 600mm .... Yes, we've got those in stock.

WOMAN: When can you deliver?

MAN: The next delivery date in your area will be on March 25th.

WOMAN: Oh. I was hoping it would arrive sooner than that. We've got a big project starting on the 15th and we really need to receive the materials by then.

MAN: OK. We can do a special delivery for £15.

WOMAN: OK. That's fine.

2

WOMAN: Good morning. Customer Service.

MARTIN: Hello. This is Martin Wright calling from Quermus.

WOMAN: Can you spell that for me?

MARTIN: Q U E R M U S.

WOMAN: Oh yes? How can I help you?

MARTIN: Well. I'm really ringing to complain about our last order.

WOMAN: OK. Can I have your account number please?

MARTIN: Yes. It's B1 387509.

WOMAN: Thank you. We seem to be having some problems with our system here so would you mind giving me some more details?

MARTIN: Right. Well, we ordered some external doors from you.

WOMAN: Do you have the order reference number there?

MARTIN: Yes, it's SM11.

WOMAN: And what was the problem with the order?

MARTIN: Well, two things really. First of all they arrived late. We were expecting them on the 25th and they finally arrived yesterday, on the 29th.

WOMAN: I'm sorry about that.

MARTIN: And then they arrived without the locks so we haven't been able to install them yet; which means the whole building project has been held up.

WOMAN: Oh dear. I am sorry. I'm afraid as the system is down I can't find out what happened but what I'll do is to contact Despatch and get the locks sent out today by special delivery. I'll also find out why the delivery arrived late and I'll call you back as soon as I have some answers. Is that OK?

MARTIN: Yes. Thank you.

Speaking focus

3c

It's very important to apologise to customers when they complain; even if it's not your fault. It's also the best way to stop someone feeling angry. Customer service staff should apologise to customers when they make the complaint and then customers should also receive a written apology after any investigation if the company is at fault.

Taking action is very important because if the customer feels nothing is being done about their problem, next time they will take their business to one of your competitors. Another important point to remember is that you may lose more than one customer in this situation because dissatisfied customers may damage your reputation by complaining about you to other potential customers. In my opinion companies should have very clear policies and procedures for dealing with complaints so that they are dealt with as efficiently as possible. That means keeping accurate records and checking that appropriate action is being taken. It's very frustrating, for example, for customers to have to keep calling a company and each time speak to a different person and have to explain the problem again and again.

Unit 12

Listening focus

1a

So how are companies using, managing and evaluating the benefits of mobile technology? For some years now, sales and marketing managers have been able to access customer-account data from locations outside the office, reps have placed orders from the road, and interactive meetings have brought together participants in multiple locations.

And yet few companies are using the technology beyond these basic applications. A majority (54%) of the 100 business-technology executives surveyed said mobile technology is used only selectively. Another 8% have almost no mobile technologies in place, although they do think it's important. The remaining 38% said their companies are trying to use mobile technology more extensively.

This contrasts strongly with employee behaviour. On average, 37% of employees constantly use mobile devices to do their jobs, and respondents expect that portion to increase to 45% within the next 12 months. Far from making their work easier, respondents felt that the increased speed and efficiency of mobile technology only added to the demands made on them at work.

Mobile devices are clearly changing people's work and communications habits, but what kind of impact are they having on companies as a whole? Surprisingly, only a minority of survey respondents have noticed any impact on their business models, while less than a third said mobile technology has increased their ability to sell products and services. Only 13% said those technologies have changed the way they market and sell products and services; and only 5% said they've expanded internationally with these technologies.

Keeping track of hundreds – or in some cases thousands – of pieces of mobile equipment seems basic, but it's no easy task. Indeed, nearly one-third of the survey respondents said their companies don't keep a proper record of how many mobile phones, laptops, blackberries and PDAs they have. Perhaps surprisingly larger companies are less likely than smaller ones to keep track of mobile equipment, according to the survey. 31% of companies also said that staff purchase of mobile equipment is not centrally controlled.

It's clearly important that control should be formalised so that one person or group is responsible. Although having a coordinated plan for networking and mobile equipment may be difficult, it's necessary so that companies can save on opportunities for volume purchases on the latest equipment. Without adequate monitoring there's also the danger of overspending.

However the survey data also showed that a far greater number than expected, 60% of the respondents, were unwilling to make further commitments to the use of mobile technology because of budget restrictions. Other reasons scored fairly high as well. Nearly half of those surveyed were worried about the return on investment. Security concerns, as you might expect, also scored fairly highly.

Speaking focus

5 Model answer

MAN: So why do you think the company wants to issue new guidelines for staff?

WOMAN: It's probably because costs are rising. I mean more and more people use mobile phones all the time. I think people are getting too dependent on their phones and this means higher bills.

MAN: Mmm. OK. So the first thing to decide is what kind of calls should be restricted.

WOMAN: Well, obviously personal calls should be restricted. It's not fair for the company to pay for their staff's personal calls.

MAN: No, but what about when staff are on business trips and need to call home? It's cheaper to use mobile phones than to pay to use hotel phones.

WOMAN: Well, the guidelines could say that staff are allowed to make one call home per day unless there is an emergency.

MAN: OK. What about international calls in general? They're so expensive when you're using a mobile phone.

WOMAN: I suppose we should have guidelines on the type of international call that's acceptable.

MAN: You mean like calling a client to confirm an appointment? That kind of thing?

WOMAN: Yes. And not calling the office at home to check some information. That can be done by email. Unless it's very urgent.

MAN: Well, even when it's urgent it's sometimes better to use email anyway. It's often easier to explain what you want when you write it down.

WOMAN: OK. How to assess staff needs for mobile phones? I suppose that means deciding which staff are out of the office often enough to justify having a mobile phone.

MAN: Yes. It depends how often they travel and where they're working. If they're working in the company's overseas office, for example, then they can be contacted there and they can use their personal mobile phone and claim for any company calls they make.

WOMAN: Yes. That's a good point. What we're looking at is whether the person's job is dependent on having a company mobile phone where the company pays for all the calls.

MAN: Yes. It's probably much cheaper to let staff claim for company calls from their own personal mobile phones.

Unit 13

Listening focus

6b

1

One point you raised was the need to build a company culture that recognises and encourages innovative ideas. I was wondering if you thought setting up a special ideas committee was the best way to get ideas for improvement or innovation from employees. Could you give any examples of the kind of company where you think this approach might work?

2

I'm sure everyone here will agree with me when I say that Jack's ideas are truly original and exciting. I was most impressed by his attention to detail and the amount of research that he and the rest of the team have done. Thank you, Jack.

3

Well, thank you for coming everybody. It's very nice to see so many of you could attend today. I know you are all very busy so I'll try to keep the presentation as brief as possible.

4

OK. We'll begin with a review of the sales figures over the last six months with an analysis of the main growth areas. Then I'll go on to discuss predicted sales for the year ahead and we'll end with a discussion on possible strategies for building growth in our main markets. If you've got any questions please do feel free to interrupt as we go along.

5

Thank you for raising that point. It's a very interesting issue and I'm not sure we have time today to go into it in any detail. However, what I can say is that despite the recent negative publicity, we're working hard to prove that we can make a positive contribution to the debate on protecting the environment and we welcome any suggestions from employees at all levels of the company.

7b

INTERVIEWER: What skills do you think you need to be a good presenter?

JAMES: I think you need a lot of confidence to be a good presenter. It's not really a skill but something that develops as you get more experience. Knowing a lot about your product or service can give you confidence so really preparing well will make you a better speaker.

INTERVIEWER: Do you think people get more nervous doing presentations in front of colleagues or customers?

JAMES: I'm not sure but I think I would feel more nervous doing a presentation for colleagues, especially if my boss was there. It's easier doing presentations for customers because they don't know you.

INTERVIEWER: Do you think you need to be a good public speaker to get to the top of a company?

JAMES: It depends on the kind of company you work for but in most cases I think this is true. I read somewhere about a survey where top American executives said that their good presentation skills had helped their careers more than any other skill.

INTERVIEWER: Do you think asking candidates to prepare a presentation for their job interview is a good idea?

JAMES: Yes. For two reasons. Firstly, it shows the interviewers if the candidate is serious about wanting the job. If they prepare well and find out a lot about the company, then they're obviously interested in the job. Secondly, it also gives you an idea of how the candidate will perform under pressure.

Unit 14

Listening focus

1b

1

Our environmental performance continued to improve this year – with reductions in waste generation and environmental incidents, fewer accidents at work and increases in recycling activities. Our renewable energy business, which concentrates on wind farm development but also invests in other forms of renewable energy, is growing fast and this year made its first real contribution to our profits. I am delighted to see our work in this area has been recognised with the company winning several external awards.

2

Our restaurant definitely appeals to a wide range of different types of customers without focusing specifically on any one. Our prices are considered reasonable and the decor and atmosphere are modern without being too 'trendy'. One of our rivals opened up with a very glamorous image and relatively high prices, obviously with the intention of targeting the 'top end' of the market. I was initially worried that we'd lose many of our customers but this doesn't seem to have happened.

3

The board comprises a chairman, two executive directors and five non-executive directors, four of whom are independent. Following the interim appointment of John Naseby as executive chairman, the roles of chairman and chief executive were separated earlier this year. We meet at least six times each year and more frequently if necessary. Directors' appointments all have to be approved by the shareholders at the annual general meeting.

4

As an international oil and gas company with operations in several countries, we are very sensitive to the diversity of social and business cultures. We know that our reputation for maintaining high standards throughout our day-to-day dealings with others is essential to our continued success. We also recognise the need to explore, produce, transport and manufacture energy products in an environmentally responsible manner, with the highest regard for the safety and health of our workforce and of course, the communities in which we operate.

Speaking focus

5 Model answer

When describing a company's values it's very important to talk about policies on employment. This is essential information for people who may want to work for the company and if they can see that the company has a good training policy or generous maternity benefits for example, they are more likely to want to work for that company. Another extremely important principle for every company is its commitment to its customers. The company should state these values very clearly so that all employees know what kind of behaviour is expected from them when dealing with customers and also for the customers to know that it can expect high standards from this company.

I think describing its vision is the first step towards a company achieving its goals. It's necessary to have these principles written down in black and white so that everyone who works for the company can share the vision and work towards achieving the same goals.

It's a good idea for a company to set itself a target for where it wants to be in five or ten years' time. Without vision and the ambition to reach targets, there's no incentive for the company to improve its performance.

Unit 15

Listening focus

2a

A survey of more than 800 managers (CEOs, HR directors and other senior managers) gives a clear picture of what sort of reorganisations companies are involved in today. Our survey shows that senior business leaders in today's environment feel that organisational change should not be a one-off activity but a regular process of adjustment and creation. But companies are experiencing major change more frequently; large UK companies are now undergoing major change about once every three years. Managers responding to this survey, experienced on average, seven corporate-wide reorganisations over the past three years.

So why do companies decide to reorganise? Respondents to the survey were asked to state the reasons behind the need to reorganise. Acquisitions were reported by 55% of respondents, closely followed by 53% reporting a decline in financial performance. In almost half of all cases, a new chief executive arrived in the 12 months before the reorganisation. A third of all companies had changed their product/service or market range over the same time period.

What are these companies hoping to achieve by reorganisation? 'Improved external effectiveness', 'improved internal effectiveness' and 'improved efficiency' show similar patterns of overall importance. Around 90% of respondents consider these as either 'important' or 'very important' aims of reorganisation. 'Improved external effectiveness', however, takes priority in many cases. It is seen as a 'very important' aim in 70% of reorganisations, compared to 54% and 59%, respectively, for improving internal effectiveness and efficiency.

It is reasonable to expect that reorganisations should be successful in achieving those aims for which they were designed. The results show that only two of the three measures of performance – external effectiveness and efficiency – were improved in more than 50% of cases. Improved internal effectiveness appears to be even more difficult to achieve. One interesting point highlighted in the survey is that sometimes, reorganisations improve performance in areas which were not originally intended. For example, efficiency is improved in 59% of reorganisations, but only in 48% of cases in which it was specifically targeted.

One key influence in shaping the nature of the reorganisation is the expertise of senior management. The survey suggests that one important way to help the senior team to manage complex reorganisations may be ideas and experiences gained from sources other than their own enterprises, with 56% of organisations saying they will make greater use of comparisons with other organisations. However, most managers did not feel using consultants would be beneficial.

Organisational change obviously has a huge impact on the workforce. Over 85% of reorganisations in the survey involve a reduction in the workforce to improve efficiency through voluntary or compulsory redundancies. But the proportion of employees affected varies substantially. Only in about 5% of reorganisations do compulsory or voluntary redundancies result in a reduction in the workforce of more than 50%. Clearly, redundancies are widespread, though the wisdom of this is at times questioned by respondents.

How far do employees have the opportunity to shape the reorganisation? In over 80% of cases, systems for communicating with employees are in place and information is given to employees affected by the organisation change. However, employees are able to participate in decisions about the organisation's future design in only 41% of reorganisations. People-centred approaches are linked with improvements in internal effectiveness, efficiency and employee-related factors. Evidence from this survey suggests organisations that invest in managing the people aspects effectively do not take longer with, or exceed their budget for reorganisation.

Speaking focus

5a

CLARE: So what do you think, Nick? Do you think this idea will be popular with staff?

NICK: Of course. Especially with women employees because it will make childcare arrangements easier. They'll have the opportunity to arrange their life the way they want to.

CLARE: Yes don't you think it will be popular with all employees? It means men can spend more time with their children too and people without children can fit studies or special hobbies around their work routine.

NICK: Maybe. But it won't be so popular with management. It'll be more difficult for them to supervise staff and make sure that work is being done properly.

CLARE: I'm not sure that's true. I think the evidence in most companies that have introduced flexible working is that staff are more productive when they can work the hours that suit them the best.

NICK: Mmm sorry, but I'm not sure I agree. I don't see how you can compare productivity like that and anyway, I wasn't talking about staff productivity I was talking about the increased workload for managers in supervising staff working flexible hours.

CLARE: Only at the beginning. Once the system is in place it'll be easy to organise ...

Answer Key

Unit 1

Listening focus 2

3a

Conversation One

1 Donoghue   2 Book Centre   3 trade show
4 014432 349876

Conversation Two

5 North   6 Klines   7 16th   8 12.30
9 07721 337065

Reading focus 1

4c

1 C   2 A   3 B   4 C   5 D   6 A   7 A   8 C
9 D   10 C   11 C   12 A

5

1 make   2 get   3 make   4 take   5 generate

Reading focus 2

7

Further to our telephone conversation yesterday, I am
<u>writing</u> to give you ~~a~~ more information about the MIS
annual <u>conference</u>.

The event will ~~be~~ take place on 22 <u>February</u> at The
Lancaster Hotel and is aimed at senior marketing personnel
<u>responsible</u> for ~~the~~ branding and brand development.

As you would expect ~~it~~ from the world's largest marketing
organisation, we have arranged for some very well-known
<u>speakers</u> so you should not ~~to~~ miss this <u>opportunity</u>.

<u>Previous</u> conferences ~~which~~ have been oversubscribed, so
you should apply for tickets now by completing ~~in~~ the
<u>enclosed</u> booking form or by visiting our website.

Writing focus

8 Model answer

Dear Chris
How was your holiday? I hope you had a nice rest.
I just wanted to let you know that the new printers I was
telling you about have arrived.
Would the 25th be convenient for me to bring one to the
office to show you?
Best wishes

Unit 2

Reading focus

1b

1 D   2 C   3 A   4 B

1c

1A   2B   3D   4D   5C   6B   7C

Writing focus

3

1 Reason for writing   2 Target reader   3 Organisation
4 Writing style

4

1 a training day for senior staff
2 Nick needs to know if Josh is free on 25 or 28
October.
3 Informal
4 Colleagues who know each other well.

5 Model answer

Hi Luke
I'm organising a meeting with some new clients to discuss
the contract. I'm hoping to resolve the main problems so we
can get the contract signed as soon as possible. Can you
give me your availability for the 15th or 16th January?
Thanks

Listening focus

6a

1 D   2 B   3 C   4 A

6b

1 C   2 D   3 B   4 A

Speaking focus

7b

Advantages: saves time, more convenient
Disadvantages: security, too many emails, some
unnecessary emails, some repeated emails

Unit 3

Writing focus

1 Model answer

Dear Jane
I think video-conferencing is a good idea. The
advantages are that we can:

- cut travel costs
- have more frequent meetings
- discuss urgent problems more easily.

However, it may be more difficult to develop working
relationships.

I think we should have meetings twice a month and
review this in six months.

Best wishes
Sam

Reading focus

2c

1 B   2 E   3 C   4 D   5 A

Listening focus

3b

1 A   2 C   3 C   4 A   5 B

Unit 4

Reading focus 1

1b

1 B   2 C   3 D   4 B   5 A   6 C   7 B   8 D
9 B   10 C

2

1 co-operatively   2 develop   3 help   4 face
5 direct   6 getting   7 demonstrate   8 developing
9 crucial   10 asset

Reading focus 2

3b

I am writing to apply for the post of Regional Manager as advertised in this week's Marketing News.

You will see from my enclosed CV that I have a three years experience as a sales rep. In the last two years I have been twice won the top sales rep award because for winning the most new contracts.

Although I do not have a degree but I am currently studying for a diploma in marketing.

I am very interested in this post because I am keen to pursue on a career in sales and feel I am ready to take on one more responsibility and would enjoy a new challenge.

I am look forward to hearing from you soon.

Writing focus

6 Model answer

Retaining Managers

Problem

The company is losing almost 50% of its graduate trainee managers in the first three years of employment. This is a serious problem for the company because we have invested a lot in the recruitment and training of these graduates. Only managers who are promoted to senior level are staying with the company for more than six years.

Solutions

Increasing salaries

Managers report a high level of dissatisfaction with their salaries and we have found that our salaries are 5% lower than our main competitors.

Promotion prospects

This is the main reason why managers are leaving. We need to review our company structure and look at new ways of promoting managers.

Other benefits

Managers report that increasing the length of holidays given depending on length of service might encourage them to stay with the company.

Listening focus

7a

1 colleagues
2 an interviewer
3 a candidate
4 colleagues

7b

1 C   2 D   3 E   4 F

Unit 5

Listening focus

1a

Conversation One
1 27th   2 early   3 airport   4 Black

Conversation Two
1 City   2 Easy delegating   3 £480   4 21st

Follow-up

1 I was wondering if …
2 Would it be OK if …
3 Would it be possible for you …
4 Is it OK …
5 Do you think you could …

Reading focus

2b

1 B   2 C   3 D   4 A   5 B   6 D   7 A

2c

1 e   2 c   3 d   4 b   5 a

Writing focus

3 Model answer

Dear Eric

I'm afraid I can't go on the trip to the USA next month. Could you go instead? I'd also like you to visit our main clients there. Can you find out if they are satisfied with our after-sales support and write a report for me when you get back?

Thanks

Unit 6

Listening focus

1a
All are receiving feedback apart from number 3.

1b
1 E   2 B   3 C   4 G

Reading focus

2b
1 A   2 D   3 C   4 A   5 D   6 B   7 B   8 A
9 C   10 B   11 D   12 A   13 B   14 C

3
achieve/reach/set/meet: goals, objectives, targets
display/show: confidence
offer/provide/give: advice, criticism, feedback, support
meet: the needs of, expectations, the challenge
take/give: a leadership role, control, responsibility, credit

Writing focus

4
PERFORMANCE REPORT: JANA BOWMAN
Jana worked as an administrative assistant supporting the sales team for three months. The work is very demanding because the team is always so busy but Jana coped with the pressure very well and developed a good relationship with each member of the team.

One of Jana's main tasks was to deal with enquiries from customers. Jana has a very professional telephone manner and was able to deal with most customer enquiries effectively.

Jana's attendance record was good; she only missed two days through sickness and she always arrived on time for work. She has a professional attitude to work which she demonstrated in her willingness to learn about the company and its products.

Although Jana's organisational skills were good, she would benefit from further training to develop her IT skills.

Unit 7

Reading focus

1a
1 Google employee
2 Google users
3 to persuade

1b
Paragraph 1: B   Paragraph 2: D
Paragraph 3: A and C

1c
1 B   2 C   3 G   4 E

Writing focus

2a
I think the ~~most~~ best way to improve your English is to listen to as much of the language as possible. Obviously, this is much easier if you ~~are~~ live in an English-speaking environment or work with ~~the~~ English-speaking colleagues but if this is not the case, you can still listen to the radio, watch TV and ~~you~~ listen to all kinds of information on the Internet. I find ~~that~~ listening to business news very helpful because the same vocabulary is used again and again so that gradually you ~~are~~ begin to recognise the words even more easily. I prefer to learn vocabulary this way, rather than studying lists, which can be quite boring. Also ~~like~~ these reports tend to be quite short, focusing on one main idea which also means you don't have to concentrate for very long. Although listening to ~~all~~ reports on the radio or ~~a~~ television is quite different to listening to a discussion in a meeting, it does help ~~in~~ to prepare you for this situation by increasing your familiarity with different accent types and with the speed at which people speak.

Listening focus

4b
1 A   2 C   3 F   4 E

Unit 8

Listening focus

1a
Conversation One
1 23rd
2 boardroom
3 new competitors
4 Helen

Conversation Two
5 19th
6 chair
7 electronic invoicing
8 consultant's report

Writing focus

2a
1 The style is too direct and may seem rude.
2 It is just a list of sentences. The information is not linked together.
3 The words 'meeting' and 'date' are repeated three times.
4 It doesn't give a clear reason for changing the date.
5 It doesn't ask Laura for confirmation that she can attend on the new date.

2b

Dear Laura

I'm afraid I have to change the date of our meeting next week. This is because one of our clients has requested an urgent meeting with me that day. Would the 6th be possible instead? Could you let me know if this is OK? Thanks

Reading focus

3c

1 C   2 A   3 A   4 C   5 B   6 D

Unit 9

Writing focus

1 Model answer

Time management workshops for new managers.
Proposal
Intrain
Advantages:

- The one-day course is preferable to limit time away from office.
- The workshops are held at the Regent Hotel which is conveniently located in the centre of town.

Disadvantages:

- The course is more expensive at £95 per person.

Recommendations

Although Intrain works out at £20 more per person I think this would be the best option because the courses are more suited to our needs. There will also be a cost-saving on travel expenses.

Reading focus

3b

1 G   2 D   3 F   4 A   5 B

Language focus

4

1 b   2 c   3 d   4 a

Listening focus

6b

1 B   2 A   3 B   4 A   5 C

6d

1 back   2 down   3 on   4 behind

Unit 10

Reading focus

1b

1 D   2 B   3 C   4 C   5 D   6 A   7 B

Self-assessment

3

launch does not collocate with *aeroplane*, *idea*, *schedule*, *train* or *presentation*.

Reading focus

4

This summer, ~~a~~ financial services company Skandia celebrated a decade as sponsor of one of the world's best-known sailing events, Cowes Week. This is an event which Skandia believes ~~so~~ represents its own brand values. Tim Sewell, Skandia's sponsorship manager explains: 'Cowes is all about ~~the~~ passion, courage and commitment and that's very much what we want to say about ourselves as an organisation.' The audience at Cowes also ~~are~~ closely match Skandia's target customers. A recent survey of Cowes Week spectators ~~did~~ showed that 60% of respondents were likely to use an independent financial adviser in the future, compared to the national average of 22% ~~each~~. In 2003, Skandia commissioned an independent evaluation of the media exposure of the brand ~~also~~ at Cowes Week and concluded ~~them~~ that they achieved an impressive 300% return on investment. Figures like these ~~too~~ explain Skandia's decision to continue sponsoring this event.

Listening focus

5b

1 B   2 F   3 G   4 E

Unit 11

Listening focus

1a

1 13th March   2 BZ38125   3 3 m 45 cm long
4 £855.90   5 25,995

1b

Conversation One
1 0093BJ   2 Unit 13b   3 CL331   4 870
5 15th March

Conversation Two
6 Quermus   7 external doors   8 25th   9 locks
10 Despatch

Reading focus

2a

B

2b

1 C   2 A   3 B   4 B   5 A   6 A   7 D   8 B
9 A   10 C   11 D   12 D

Writing focus

3 Model answers

Dear Andrew

I think the transit times for sending goods by road are getting more unreliable. I think it's a good idea to find out about ships or trains. Can you write a report about this? I want you to write about the costs and transit times for a few freight forwarding companies.

Thanks

Nick

Dear Andrew

I'm concerned about the increased unreliability of transit times for transportation by road and I'd like to find out about using alternative methods of transport. Could you write a report on all possible options? I'd like you to include information on the costs and transit times for several freight forwarding companies.

Thanks

Nick

5b

1 b   2 a   3 d   4 c

Unit 12

Listening focus

1b

1 A   2 B   3 C   4 A   5 C   6 A

Reading focus

3

Presentation on mobile technology use

According to a recent survey, most ~~of~~ companies:

- are only using mobile technology in a limited way
- have noticed no impact on business models
- keep records of how much mobile equipment they ~~are~~ own.

Many companies are prevented from ~~having~~ further investment in mobile technology because of budget restrictions. However, other companies feel the high investment is ~~only~~ worth it because of the guaranteed return on investment.

The survey showed that employees believe the use of mobile technology will increase ~~up~~ slightly. However, employees feel improved communications ~~it~~ also mean they will be expected to work faster.

Having a coordinated plan is ~~too~~ important because:

- companies can get ~~more~~ better discounts on purchases of mobile equipment
- money is not ~~been~~ wasted on unnecessary equipment.

Writing focus

4

Mobile phone use

Introduction

The aim of this report was to find out why the company's mobile phone bills have been increasing and to look at ways of making savings.

Findings

- More mobile phones are being issued to junior managers than to those more senior.
- The number of international calls made has increased dramatically.
- More personal calls are being made. 32% of all calls made are to family or friends.
- More than half of all calls are made on business trips (58%).

Recommendations

A new policy should be drawn up:

- Only junior managers who travel a lot should be given mobile phones.
- The number of personal calls managers are allowed to make should be restricted.
- Managers should only make international calls when it is urgent.

Unit 13

Reading focus

1d

1 C   2 A   3 D   4 D   5 B   6 B

Language focus

3

1 convinced/advised/persuaded: to ... somebody to do something
2 influenced: to influence something
3 suggested/recommended: + ing

Writing focus

5 Model answer

BILLY DRYDEN: FEEDBACK ON PRESENTATION

Content:

You spent too long on the introduction talking about the company's history. The main focus of the presentation was on the company's future so you only needed to talk briefly about its history.

Although some of the slides were very interesting, there were far too many which made it difficult for the audience to remember all the information.

Body language:

I was very pleased to see that you did not rely on reading from your notes but you are still not making eye-contact with the audience. Remember this is very important for establishing rapport.

You are still moving your hands and arms too much which makes you look nervous. Standing straight and keeping your hands in one position will help you to look and feel more confident.

Listening focus

6a
A 4   B 2   C 6   D 5   E 3   F 8   G 7   H 1

6b
1 D   2 C   3 A   4 H   5 G

Unit 14

Listening focus

1b
1 H   2 C   3 B   4 E

Reading focus

2c
1 E   2 G   3 B   4 D   5 C

Language focus

3b
1 mainstream 2 seamless solution 3 pioneering 4 core competence

Writing focus

4c Model answer
We are pleased to announce a new funding scheme for employees who are interested in studying for a business qualification.
The aim of this scheme is to ensure staff have the opportunity to develop their skills.
All employees who have been with the company for at least two years may apply.

4d Model answer
We are delighted to announce a new award for best employee of the year. The aim of the award is to recognise and reward staff who have shown commitment to their colleagues and to the company.
The award is open to all employees on grades A–G.
The winner will be given a two-week holiday to the Caribbean.

Unit 15

Reading focus

1
1 C   2 B   3 D   4 A   5 B   6 C   7 B   8 D
9 A   10 C   11 A   12 B   13 A   14 B   15 D

Listening focus

2a
1 C   2 A   3 C   4 B   5 C   6 B   7 C

Writing focus

3 Model answer
Report on the success of flexible working.
Successes
Since the introduction of flexible working in 2002, the number of staff choosing to work flexible hours has doubled. One of the main reasons for this is that flexible working is very popular with women. Flexible working allows women with young children to work around their childcare commitments.
The number of managers now in favour of flexible working has increased dramatically. This is because it is now clear that flexible working does not decrease productivity.
Failures
60% of full-time male employees report that flexible working would damage their career. Although attitudes among managers are changing, there is still a tendency among male employees to see long hours as a sign of commitment.
The small increase in flexible workers in 2004 is due to poor transport links at off-peak times.